THE DESTINY OF A KING

THE DESTINY OF A KING

GEORGES DUMÉZIL

TRANSLATED BY ALF HILTEBEITEL

THE UNIVERSITY OF CHICAGO PRESS
CHICAGO AND LONDON

Originally published as part three of *Mythe et épopée*, vol. 2:
Types épiques indo-européens: un héros, un sorcier, un roi,
© Editions Gallimard, 1971.

The University of Chicago Press, Chicago 60637
The University of Chicago Press, Ltd., London

Printed in the United States of America
International Standard Book Number: 0-226-16975-8
Library of Congress Catalog Card Number: 73-75311

To the members of the Haskell Lecture Committee (1969):
Jerald C. Brauer, Robert E. Streeter, Mircea Eliade,
Joseph M. Kitagawa, and Charles H. Long

To the faculty and students of the University of Chicago

To Zwi Werblowsky

Prefatory Note

The following study, outlined partially in three lectures at the Collège de France in January 1966, took form in six Haskell Lectures given at the University of Chicago in October and November 1969. Some complementary comparative research was set forth at Chicago in several seminars (October–December 1969); other material was presented in lectures at Philadelphia and Los Angeles (February 1970).

With warm appreciation I thank Alf Hiltebeitel, to whom this careful and competent version of my French text is due, as well as Winston Davis, who assisted me unselfishly during the time of my lectures in Chicago.

CONTENTS

INTRODUCTION

The comparison of the Indian Yama, son of Vivasvat, with his Iranian homonyn Yima,[1] son of Vīvañhat, runs up against an initial difficulty. Formulated briefly, Yima corresponds to Yama in only a confined portion of his adventures and functions. For the rest, the larger portion of his career not only bears no relation to what we know of Yama, but hardly even seems compatible with his type. Let us begin by looking at the various ways in which this father-son pair appears.[2]

The Vedic Vivasvat presents himself as a contradiction: at once a man, the ancestor of the human race, and a god, the eighth and last of the Ādityas, or sovereign gods. This second ranking, alluded to by *ṚV* X,72,8 and 9, is enlarged upon in several Brāhmaṇas and explained as a sort of original sin by Aditi, the Ādityas' mother. She had given birth, two by two, to the six Ādityas proper—Mitra and Varuṇa, then two auxiliaries for each—by eating piously and humbly the remainder of some gruel which had first been offered to the Sādhyas, the primordial gods. But when it came time for a fourth try, hoping for an even greater result, she ate the initial share before serving the gods. The outcome was that one of the two children, Indra, rose up proudly toward the sky and joined company with the Ādityas (he was to be "the seventh Āditya"), whereas the other fell, in the form of the "dead egg," Mārtāṇḍa. It required the intervention of the Ādityas to give him life and form: thus he became Vivasvat. But they gave him their aid only on the condition that he and those born from him "would be for them," that is, that they would sacrifice to them. Vivasvat thus became the first sacrificer, and those men, his descendants, who sacrifice as he did are protected by the Ādityas. In this way they postpone their death, the moment when they will be gathered up by Yama, son of Vivasvat.

The Avestan Vīvaṅhat reveals no such complication or ambiguity: he is only a man of long ago who was the first to sacrifice and who, as reward for this beautiful invention, was enabled to have a son Yima, under whom death was postponed for a long time

It may be that the Avesta presents the tradition in its most ancient Indo-Iranian form, and that the situation was complicated in late Vedic texts—the tenth book of the *R̥g Veda, Brāhmaṇas*—by making the ancestor of humanity one of the minor sovereign gods. The ancient list of the six Ādityas would thus have been prolonged: in overseeing the mysteries of the cosmos. *Váruṇa* and his two assistants *Dákṣa* and *Áṃśa* would, on the "Varuṇian plane," find their ranks completed by a *god* not properly Āditya, but particularly brilliant (*Índra*); and in maintaining close ties with us men, *Mitrá* and his two assistants *Aryamán* and *Bhága*[3] would be joined on the "Mitrian plane" by an exceptional *man* (*Vivasvat*). Be that as it may, whether one regards him as a man who is both exemplary and promoted to immortality or as a heterogeneous sovereign god, Vivasvat, like his Avestan counterpart, draws mention above all for his part as primal sacrificer.

Further, it was around Vivasvat, ancestor of mankind, and his son Yama that the Vedic Indians and probably even the Indo-Iranians had organized their ideas on life and death. One can summarize the Vedic doctrine in a few words: Vivasvat, whether by his sacrificial merits or through his connection with the Ādityas, has been relieved of the necessity of dying which fell to him when he was born as Mārtāṇḍa; on the contrary, his son Yama is dead, and, following him, we all die too. Let us also expect them to render different services. Under the protection of Vivasvat, we ask not for an impossible immortality on earth but for a life as long as possible and a natural death as late as possible; with the help of Yama, "the first to die," our "guide in death," soon "king of the realm of the dead," we hope for as happy a survival as possible in the beyond—this happiness being subject to different conceptions which varied from age to age and which seem to have remained rather vague throughout Vedic times. This is the theology expressed in all those parts of the hymns which treat the relations of Vivasvat and Yama to death. One may think first of the famous prayer in strophe 62 of *Atharva Veda* 18,3 (following strophe 61, which asks Vivasvat for security, abundance in men, cows, and horses):

> Let Vivasvat set us in non-mortality; let death go away; let what is non-mortal come to us; let [him] defend these men until old age; let not their life-breaths go to Yama.[4]

Then *AV* 18,2,32, where the poet reassures himself by proclaiming that he is ready on either side, for this world or for the other:

> Yama beyond, below Vivasvat—beyond that do I see nothing whatever; upon Yama is placed my sacrifice; Vivasvat is extended upon the worlds.

And again *AV* 18,3,13, which provides Yama with a definition that Alfred Hillebrant tried vainly to discredit, attempting to distinguish "mortal" from "man."

> Him who died first of mortals, who went forth first to that world, Vivasvat's son, assembler of mankind, king Yama, honor ye with oblation.

The Vedic Indians had to pose themselves the problem of the origin of death: if Vivasvat, for one reason or another—whether as first sacrificer or thanks to the compassion of the Ādityas—was able to escape mortality, how is it that this son Yama and especially the rest of us humans have had to submit to it? Insofar as Yama is concerned, it seems that the interested party himself has been granted the decision. And as for mankind, Yama has no part in the events which led to our mortal condition. As we learn from the lengthy exposition of the *Bṛhaddevatā* (6,162–7,7), Tvaṣṭṛ, the divine artisan, had given his daughter Saraṇyū in marriage to Vivasvat, and their first children were the twins Yama and his sister Yamī (*yama* is an old word which signifies "twin"). But then, without the knowledge of her husband, Saraṇyū created a feminine form like her own, in which the deceived Vivasvat engendered Manu, the father of humanity. If we are after an entirely coherent picture, we may suppose—although nowhere is this connection made explicit—that Yama has chosen mortality freely so as to open a "realm" in the afterworld where he may welcome his half-brother Manu's descendants, the human race, whose life involves death in consequence of his mother's trick. In any case, in the funerary hymns of the *Ṛg Veda*, such is his function: where Yama lives, in a remarkable association with Varuṇa, there—even if no one can be precise on the location—go the good ārya at death to continue their terrestrial lives comfortably.

In this sense he is a king, for he is called "king" already in the hymns, and the title was so firmly attached to him that, in branching off from Indian tradition and making him their chief god, the Kafirs of the Hindukush incorporated it into his name: *Imra*, that is, *Yama-rājan*.[5] But neither in the Vedic epoch nor later has he ever been thought of as "ruling" or as "having ruled" at any time whatsoever over a "kingdom" of our world. In the later traditions, all traces of a human origin disappear: in the epic, the king of the dead is a god on equal terms with the others and, as one of the protectors of the four cardinal points—of the five, if the zenith is included—he has a palace as splendid and of the same style as those of his four associates, the gods Indra, Varuṇa, Kubera, and, elevated over all the exalted figure referred to as "Grandfather."

On the contrary, in the *Avesta* and in all the posterior literature, Yima is above all a terrestrial king, the third and last of a prestigious succession—Haošyaṅha Paraδāta, Taxma Urupi, Yima Xšaēta. He is, moreover, a universal king, and one whose title—for *xšaēta* signifies "king" and not "luminous," as it has long been rendered[6]—is also incorporated into his name, producing the Pahlavi Yamšēt, the *J̌amšīd* of the Persian tradition of the Muslim period. His entire life, full of adventures which lead him from an unheard-of prosperity to the most terrible catastrophe, is terrestrial, and it is impossible to align it in any way with the funerary mission of the Indian Yama. On one essential point the two careers are even opposed: during Yima's reign, says the *Avesta*, not only were sickness and old age suspended, but death itself.

Only one episode in Yima's life, poorly connected with the rest, seems to be the Zoroastrian transformation of an Indo-Iranian tradition about Yama conceived of as lord of the dead. Like the authors of comedies and novels who, from one edition to the next, reverse the direction of the last turn of events to provide a "good" ending for an intrigue which first ended "badly," the *Avesta* mingles two conceptions of Yima's reign that are difficult to reconcile.[7] In one, he ends his earthly existence with an enormous sin—a lie, or pride, or revolt against God—which makes him lose for good, with no possibility of retrieving them, his throne, the sign of divine election, and even his life. In the other, he is charged by God with a mission that would normally have to remove him from our world and call him, in a kind of Beyond, to a life which, if not of unlimited duration, is at least much prolonged and without mishap. He is charged with constructing a subterranean enclosure[8] where he is to install, to put in safekeeping in anticipation of a terrible cosmic winter, selected specimens of humanity and of the good creation. And if this winter does not mark the beginning of a true "end of the world" as the great Scandinavian winter, the *fimbulvetr*, seems to have done in concurrence with the Ragnarök, it at least marks a grave crisis occurring at the end of the "millennium of Zoroaster."[9] One fine day, Ahura Mazdā warned Yima that there were going to be terrible winters with snows so heavy that, upon melting, they would submerge the earth. He commanded him to construct a *vara*, a (subterranean) enclosure with specified dimensions, and to bring to it, in pairs, the seeds of the best of each living species, especially the human. Let him make the waters flow there, put grasslands there, and then, says the Great God, there will be inexhaustible food there, but no deformities or physical or mental illnesses (22–30). Finally, so as to set the boundaries of the parts of the *vara*, Ahura Mazdā gives Yima a gold object, the nature of which is discussed by the exegetes (30). Yima carries out these orders from point to point, and thus he is able to construct the marvelous enclosure (31–38). The following dialogue (39–41) completes the description:

"Creator of the bodily world, O holy one! What, O Ahura Mazdā, are the lights which shine there, in the *vara* which Yima built?"

"Natural lights and artificial lights. The stars, moon, and sun are seen to set and to rise one time [only in the year]. And a year seems but a day. Every forty years each human couple gives birth to a couple, male and female. And the same for the animal species. And there men live the very best of lives in the *vara* which Yima made."[10]

This happy enclosure of the beyond, though presented not as a land of the dead but, on the contrary, as the refuge of the living whose destiny is to escape a cataclysm, is very likely a prolongation of the Indo-Iranian conception which in India, more simply, made Yama the chief of the kingdom of the dead. The anomaly is that even though he is charged by God with building the enclosure and setting up and organizing in it the society and even the economy of the elect, Yima is not designated as their chief and seems to lose interest in the enclosure he has prepared. The reasons for this elimination may be conjectured.

First of all, Zoroaster has intervened. As soon as he has heard the long description of the *vara*, the prophet asks his God:

42. "Creator of the bodily world, O holy one! Who brought the Mazdean religion into the *vara* which Yima made?" And Ahura Mazdā said: "It is the bird Karšiptar, O Spitama Zaraθuštra."

43. "Creator of the bodily world, O holy one! Who is their master and judge?" And Ahura Mazdā said: "It is Urvatat̰nara the third son of Zaraθuštra, O Zaraθuštra, and yourself, you who are Zaraθuštra."

In this, as in other circumstances of his career—for example the establishment of social classes through his sons[11]—Yima has thus conceded his place to the prophet of the new religion. It is certainly conceivable that before Zoroaster and his reform, before the imperialistic reinterpretation which his disciples made of Indo-European myths and legends, the heroic builder of the enclosure would have continued until the end of time to preside there over the society he had brought together. Furthermore, it is reasonable to suggest that in the primitive tradition, just as the Vedic Yama's realm was a sojourn for the dead, the enclosure could have provided a destination for the "good" dead of the ārya.

The second reason for the dispossession of Yima is probably that a prolonged stay in the enclosure he had constructed—a happy existence, without definite limit, in another world—would have contradicted the rest, or at least the end, of his legend: sin, dethronement, brief period of disgrace, cruel death. To say it again, there is nothing about this final statement that has any analogue in the Vedic or post-Vedic dossier on Yama.

Aside from this Iranian tradition concerning the enclosure which, although it has a likely Indian homologue,[12] shows the great divergences we have just underlined; aside also from the identical names of the two fathers (Vivasvat, Vīvaṅhat) and the particular, but inverse, relations of Yima and Yama to death and its suspension, there are three traits concerning civil status in which a correspondence still holds between the two figures. First of all, their name, with its meaning of "twin"; then the presence, beside them, of a sister, the predictable "girl twin" whose name is diversely derived from theirs—in Vedic India Yamī, in Iran, the Pahlavi form Yimāk; and finally the relations which they have with this sister: in a conversational R̥gVedic hymn, the Indian figure indignantly repulses his sister's repeated propositions of incest, while in the Pahlavi texts, resting on an Avestan tradition, the Iranian Yima consummates incest with his sister, supplying the first example of marriage among near kin which Zoroastrianism regarded as the noblest form of marriage.[13] Despite the similarities, however, there is considerable divergence of detail, and not only as a result of the two societies' contrasting views of incest: in Iran the event takes place during the year of miserable and secret survival which the sinful Yima leads during his dethronement and punishment.

One thing about this apparently hopeless dossier suggests that we look at it from a new point of view. Those of Yima's adventures —the most considerable portion—which seem incompatible with the type and function of Yama form a coherent ensemble and make of him the best example of what Arthur Christensen has called a "first king." As such he is inserted, at the third and last position, in the earliest period of the "history" of Iran: universal king, civilizer, organizer, beneficiary—until his sin—of a special protection from God. Now although the frameworks and the intentions differ, we have shown elsewhere[14] that certain lines of comparison can be drawn between the ways that the inventors of Iranian "history" and the Indian authors of the *Mahābhārata* epic composed their early dynastic traditions. On this basis we are led to the possibility that Yima, in his role as universal sovereign, *may* have, under other names, one or several counterparts among the most ancient ancestors of the Pāṇḍavas. Accordingly, the idea naturally arises that the last of the "universal" kings in the Indian and the Iranian lists, Yayāti and Yima-J̌amšīd, *may* both have inherited epic material deriving in part from a common source. This is the hypothesis that we are about to test. In addition, on the maternal side the Pāṇḍavas have another ancestor, Vasu Uparicara, whose surname evokes one of the most celebrated privileges of "J̌amšīd," one, moreover, for which neither Yama nor Yayāti presents an equivalent. We shall also seek to appreciate how far this new correspondence extends and what consequences it holds for an understanding of the exploit of Yima.

1

YAYĀTI AND HIS SONS

1. The Divisions of the Earth

Since antiquity, the import and value of the stereotyped R̥gVedic expressions "the five lands," "the five peoples," have been open to discussion, and they will continue to be so for a long time to come.[1] The most sensible and best-reasoned interpretation is that which Bernfried Schlerath proposed in an excursus of his book of 1960, *Das Königtum im Rig- und Atharvaveda.*[2]

Despite certain indigenous explanations which referred not only to men and the earth but to divine characters and mythical worlds, these words surely have to do with five human groups. The expression is sometimes equivalent to the totality of the ārya (for example, when it is said that the five peoples are devoted to Mitra, *R̥V* 3,59,8; sacrifice or pray to Agni, 6,11,4; and 10,45,6; ask for the help of Indra, 10,53,4 and 5; or prepare the soma, 9,65,23), sometimes, in a comprehensive way, to the whole of humanity living on the earth (for example, when it is said that in a day Dawn tours the five lands, 5,75,4, or awakens them, 7,79,1; or in certain standardized formulas where the accusatives *páñca carṣaṇī́ḥ* and *víśvāḥ . . . carṣaṇī́ḥ* are used equivalently). This double interpretation is not contradictory: it was the ārya who primarily interested the poets, and in many cases the ārya constituted the only "humanity" which concerned them.

The division into five probably corresponded to an ancient conception, purely terrestrial,[3] of the five *díśaḥ*, or *pradíśaḥ*, the directions of the world, that is, the four cardinal points and the center,[4] a natural conception found widely on every continent.[5]

When the expression was taken in its most comprehensive sense, the center might refer to the ārya, surrounded on all sides by the barbarians (cf. the Chinese expression "Empire of the Middle"); when it was restricted to the ārya, the center, as occurs frequently, would presumably be the land, the particular land or clan of the poet or of his royal employers, surrounded by the rest of the nation, whether friendly or hostile.

It is likely that this conception of the world and its occupation was even part of the Indo-Iranian tradition. To be sure, the Zoroastrian texts[6] divide the world into seven parts, the seven *kišvar* (Avestan *karšvar*); but beneath these, in the very names and the distribution of the "sevenths," one perceives a division into five with the four cardinal points and the center. Put simply, it is a question of a conception that is not purely terrestrial, but which has been enlarged, cosmicized. As Arthur Christensen says:

> The central *kišvar*, the *x^{v}aniras* (Avestan *x^{v}aniraθa*), comprises the entire world, surrounded by the Vourukaša ocean, the other *kišvars* being fabulous worlds inaccessible to man. It is only with divine assistance—or rather, as others claim, with the aid of the *dēv*—that one can cross over the ocean which separates these *kišvars* from the *x^{v}aniras*. Later the conception of the *kišvars* changes. The *x^{v}aniras* is no longer surrounded by the ocean; rather, it constitutes only half of the earth, the six other *kišvars*, each of which is equal in extent to Sīstān, altogether form the other half. The *x^{v}aniras*, whose center is Fars [= Persia, properly speaking], is separated from the other divisions of the world in part by the ocean, in part, on the northern border, by high mountains and forests. Here the *x^{v}aniras* has evidently been identified with eastern Asia (Iran, Mesopotamia, Syria, etc.) which, in antiquity and in the middle ages, through the vicissitudes of political history, formed a whole from the point of view of political economy and intellectual life; and the other *kišvars* are no longer mythical worlds, but little or unknown regions of the earth.[7]

The six peripheral *kišvars* mentioned in the *Bundahišn* are distributed among the four cardinal points in a remarkable manner: one (Arzah) in the west, one (Savah) in the east, two (Vōrūbaršt and Vōrūgaršt) in the north, and two (Fratatafš and Vitatafš) in the south. We note that the names for the northern pair are differentiated only in the initial consonant of the second member, while the names for the southern couplet differ only in the initial prefix.

This suggests that a five-term system[8] has been made to fit into another, seven-term system, perhaps under the influence of Babylonian thought in which the number seven played such an important role.[9]

Another line of thought, brilliantly developed in 1961 by Alwyn and Brinley Rees,[10] induces us to place the conception still farther back. In order to designate the great territorial divisions, the "provinces" of their island, the Irish consistently used the word *cóiced*, "fifth," for which there existed—concurrently, it seems—two geographical interpretations. According to one, based on historical situations, the five *cóiceds* took roughly the shape of triangles whose bases formed the contiguous coastal portions and whose apexes, opposite the bases, came together approximately at the middle of the island: Ulster to the north, Connaught to the west, Leinster to the east, and, to the south, two Munsters, the western and eastern, the latter of very reduced size and uncertain autonomy. According to the other interpretation, Ulster, Connaught, Leinster, and a single Munster left one place, at the center of the island, for the little territory of Meath (Mide), which in prehistoric times contained Tara, the capital of the *ardrí*, the "supreme king" of Ireland. This second, more abstract, interpretation of the Fifths of the island has led to, and has remained tied to, certain very interesting speculations of which Alwyn and Brinley Rees have made an admirable study[11] and which, bringing in the three Indo-European functions complemented by a fourth term and crowned by the Royal Power, probably derive from a Druidic doctrine. In the course of a narrative filled with theoretical statements,[12] a man named Fontan is asked by a supernatural being "O Fontan, how has our island been divided, what things were found there [that is, were found in each of its divisions]?" Fontan replies: "Knowledge is in the west, Battle in the north, Prosperity in the east, Music in the South, Royalty in the center." And the supernatural being, in turn, develops this information in a somewhat confused manner according to that Irish rhetoric of *amplitudo* (which bears some resemblance to Indian rhetoric), overloading each of the Fifths with qualities that do not conform to this schema but which allow it to subsist in the main and, at several points, reinforce it.[13]

Neither the Iranian *kišvars* nor the Vedic "five lands" are similarly characterized by functional values. In India, in order to glimpse such a connection between divided lands and the principles of the social functions, we must await the emergence of a somewhat unstable conception, that of the *lokapālas*, the regent gods of the cardinal points.[14] Varuṇa, the ancient magical sovereign (reduced in the epic to the patronage of the waters); Indra, the celestial warrior (king of the gods in the epic); Kubera, a lord of riches; and Yama, the ruler of the land of the dead, generally divide up the four directions in the following order: west, north, east, south. As can be seen, the first three of these allocations take us back to the functional mapping of Ireland.

With or without functional coloration, a geographical division of the world or of the land readily calls for a legend of origin, of which the most simple type is a partition among brothers.[15] Where distinct origins are attributed by the legends to the two kinds of divisions (social functions and provinces), it may happen that one of the two is established by a generation of brothers, and the other by a second generation. The typical case is the Scythians' legend of origin, according to the fourth book of Herodotus: the four sons of Targitaos appear to be the ancestors of functional groups or types (king-priests, warriors, and two kinds of stock breeders); then one of this first group of brothers, the king, apportions the full extent of all the Scythian lands among his own three sons.[16]

Although no legend of this type, settling the territorial boundaries and providing functional definitions at one stroke, has been transmitted concerning the Irish *coiceds*,[17] examples have for some time been recognized concerning other points in the Indo-European world, in which the two kinds of divisions, equally linked together, are explained by a partition among brothers. Here, however, it is generally a question not of "fifths" but of "thirds," the latter permitting the division of the world (or of lands of interest, national or otherwise) to conform exactly to the original terms of the Indo-European structure of functions, but by way of compensation, detaching it from the structure of the cardinal points. Let us think, for instance, of the tradition of the continental Germans at the beginning of our era concerning the three sons of Mannus, son of

Tuisto; the onomastic skeleton is all that remains, but it is precise.

With regrettable brevity, Tacitus notes[18]—referring to "the old poems which serve these peoples as history and annals"—that the ancestor of the Germans was called Mannus and that the three parts of the Germanic world owed their names to his sons: those "nearest the Ocean" are called *Ingaeuones* (*Inguaeones*), those "of the middle" are the *Herminones*, and all the rest *Istaeuones* (*Istuaeones*). It is a question, then, of a division into roughly parallel bands, from the northern seas to the southern mountains; and the eponymous figures, the sons of Mannus themselves, who can be perceived under the ethnic names, correspond to the three terms of the divine trifunctional triad which still dominated the Scandinavian pantheon at the end of paganism: Freyr, the great Vanic god of fecundity and prosperity, is called *Yngvifreyr* (**Ingu̯i̯afrau̯i̯az*[19]) and the dynasty which refers itself to him is that of the Ynglingar; Óðinn, the magical sovereign, bears the surname *jörmunr* (**ermunaz*); and, as the radical of Istaeuones (Pliny: Istri[an]ones), if it is not to be found in a surname of the powerful combative god Þórr, it derives from a root which, in Indo-Iranian as in Old Icelandic, has produced a number of technical words for the warrior function. Thus, in Sanskrit we have *iṣirá* "strong, unbridled," epithet of the Maruts, the troop of celestial young warriors who accompany Indra;[20] in Avestan, Aēšma, a demon of cruel violence, probably owes his name to the same root; and in Old Icelandic there is the verb *eiskra*, which characterizes the state of furor of the *berserkir*, warriors of supernatural powers.[21]

In Iran, the legends of the origin and peopling of the *kišvars* in their mythical, cosmic form are entirely different and are the results of highly elaborated reflections. In the Iranian tradition it is at another point, allegedly historical, that one observes the legend just referred to, which Arthur Christensen compared with that of the sons of Mannus and which Marijan Molé has elucidated so well.[22] According already to a Pahlavi text, the ancient Θraētaona, Frētōn-Feridūn—who is inserted in the list of kings—conducts a partition of the habitable world among his three sons, in accordance with the three functions. It will suffice to recall here the most ancient variant of the account.

Three sons were born to Frētōn: Salm, Tōz, and Ērič were their names. He called all three together to say to them: "I will divide up the entire world between you; let each of you tell me what seems good to him so that I may give it to him." Salm asked for great riches [*vas-hērīh*], Tōz for valor [*takīkīh*], and Ērič, who had the Kavian Glory [*xvarrah i kayān:* the Avestan *x*^{v}*arənah*] upon him, for law and religion (*dāt u dēn*). Frētōn said: "May what each of you has asked for come to him." To Salm he gave the land of Rome [*zamīk i Hrōm*] down to the sea coast; to Tōz he gave Turkestan and the desert down to the sea coast; and Ērānšaθr [the Iranian realm] and India, down to the sea, fell to Ērič. At one moment [. . . ? . . .] Frētōn lifted the crown from his head and put it on the head of Ērič, saying: "My Glory is established on the head of Ērič until the morning of the Renovation of all the living world; O honored one, may the royalty and sovereignty over the children of Tōz and Salm belong to your children."[23]

The three parts of the world—the west (Rome) with riches; the north and east (Turkestan and the deserts) with martial turbulence; the south (Iran and India) with religion, law, and the supreme royalty besides—are conceived here as adjoining each other at their peaks and extending all three "down to the sea," that is, down to the peripheral ocean. There is no "center": the supreme royalty belongs to the land of the "first function." The principal interest in this account is in the manner in which the partition is made. It makes use of a sort of examination in which the three sons have their separate natures revealed in the responses they make to a single question. And from these answers, the father sends two away from Iran, to the less attractive "thirds," and reserves the good "third," with the sovereignty marked on the head by the *x*^{v}*arənah*,[24] for the youngest, who has made the most noble response. Naturally, the frustrated elder sons are hardly inclined to accept such a decision.

Seeing how things had transpired, Salm and Tōz said: "What has our father Frētōn done, who has not bestowed the authority on his oldest son, nor on his next-born son, but on his youngest son?" They sought a favorable moment and killed their brother Ērič.

But it is nonetheless Ēric's descent that is installed on the Iranian throne. The two other thirds of the world, the Roman and Turanian, are thereby left to attack it in interminable and, when all is considered, fruitless wars.

2. Yayāti and the Partition of the World

We have briefly reviewed these generally accepted comparative points because a similar story about the partition of the "world," in the first book of the *Mahābhārata*, forms the episode which introduces the legend of Yayāti.[25] This king, as I hope to show, corresponds closely to the flexible but hardly illusory notion which Christensen has labeled "the figure of the first king." The designation does not imply that kings of this type would necessarily or generally be the actual first king, but rather that other orderings of the same "historical" material could readily have made them so; and above all, that, whatever their rank, they institute all or part of the great classifications of social life and often, by extension, the great divisions of the earth and of humanity. It is in these capacities that Yayāti, like Frētōn, apportions the world between his five sons, although with no functional overtones.

Between his five sons: for it is the Vedic formula of the "five peoples," reinterpreted to suit the geography of the times, that provides the ground plan for the division. To the extent to which the lay of the lands and waters permits, this division is made between four peripheral sections and one central section—the latter being the most elevated in dignity, India at its most arya, if one may say so, the future kingdom of the Pāṇḍavas.

With no functional overtones: indeed, the number five, applied to a group of brothers, would scarcely permit such a configuration. The number four would have allowed it, with the king at the center and each of the three arya (noble) functions—the sacred, the martial, the economic—on the circumference. With five terms things were different. It was obviously not desirable to claim that the *śūdras*, the non-arya class which is subordinated rather than added to the three arya classes, had participated on the same plane as the others in a partition between brothers who were unequal in qualities but equal in rank.

Finally, when the father addresses himself to his five sons, it is not, as with Frētōn, to examine them calmly, in order to know objectively the depths of their natures before distributing, as best he could, the proper lot to each. On the contrary, he is most interested in the answers they give to a question which is in fact a request.

As a result, the dismissal of each of the four elder brothers to lands outside India is not a mediocre assignment pursuant to an adequate response, but the punishment for an abusive refusal.

A fatal course of events has drawn upon Yayāti the wrath of his wife and, at her request, the curse of his father-in-law, who was a sorcerer. With obvious reluctance, Yayāti has had to marry Devayānī, the imperious daughter of Kāvya Uśanas. Moreover, the latter has instructed Yayāti that Devayānī must be accompanied to her marriage residence by the charming princess Śarmiṣṭhā, who, having once offended Devayānī, had been demanded and received by the latter as a slave. Human nature, however, has its own way, aided by a subtle argument. And so, while Yayāti has two little princes by his legitimate spouse, he has secretly fathered three sons by her slave. When the secret is discovered, there is a terrific row, and Yayāti's dreadful father-in-law condemns the guilty husband to become old instantly: the young man is brought nigh to ruin. However, he begs for mercy, and his sentencer allows him not a reduction of the punishment but the right to seek someone who will take it for him:

> My word cannot be in vain: even now you are beset with decrepitude. But if you so desire, transfer this decrepitude to another.[26]

Yayāti is rich in sons, who he has reason to think are devoted and grateful. He thus demands more precise information about the favor he is about to obtain:

> O brahman, let it be commanded by you that the son of mine who gives me his youth shall enjoy, altogether, royalty, virtue, and fame![27]

Kāvya Uśanas consents:

> It will suffice for you to think of me, and you may transfer your decrepitude, without sin, as you wish. That son of yours who will give you his youth shall be king. He shall also have long life, fame, and numerous progeny!"[28]

In an emulator of Euripides, such a situation would have inspired a series of scenes, attitudes, and varied discourses, or lively discussions between father and sons,[29] in which the refusal to take on old age would each time be justified by well-balanced arguments. But the Indian poets did not fear monotony, and, besides, in this particular case, are they not closer to the quite simple truth, closer to each of us? There is no *De senectute*, no sophism able to make us love or choose old age. The four scenes in which, in the order of their births, the two sons of Devayānī and the two older of the three sons of Śarmiṣṭhā—that is, Yadu and Turvasu, then Druhyu and Anu—refuse to exchange their age for that of their father, contain nothing unexpected, nothing piquant, nothing refined. To each, the request is presented flatly, almost in the same terms: "Take to yourself this decrepitude of mine so that I may enjoy life with your vigor. When a thousand years have elapsed, I will return it to you."[30] To which Yadu responds, without hesitation, that old age involves many inconveniences as to drinking and eating; that it is accompanied by white hair, melancholy, flaccid muscles, wrinkles all over the body, deformities, weakness, emaciation, incapacity to work; that it inspires aversion, even in those who are close; and that therefore he does not want it and can only advise his father to address himself to others.[31] More sober, Turvasu is no less peremptory: old age prohibits pleasures, destroys strength, beauty, intelligence, memory, and, finally, life itself.[32] Druhyu makes the added point that an old man can no longer benefit from elephants, horses, or women, and that he stammers when speaking.[33] Finally Anu declares himself disgusted by those fallen beings who eat like infants, soil themselves constantly, and can no longer even make libations on the fire altar at the proper times.[34] It would be vain to search all this for any kind of order, say, for four particular orientations of repugnance. The forms of punishment which the unappreciated father levels upon his sons, even if the last three seem adjusted to the answers which provoked them, do not lend themselves to a further classification, functional or otherwise.[35] To Yadu, he says that his descendants will always be *arājyabhāj*, that is, "without the enjoyment of royalty." Turvasu is told that he will be a king over men who fail to observe, especially in their marriages, the statutes of the *varṇas*, but live in the manner of animals and do not hesitate to take the wives of their spiritual masters: in short, that he will rule over sinners and Mlecchas. To Druhyu he announces that he will never be king except in name,[36] and that he will live with his companions in a land without roads, where no horses, elephants, or asses, no animal or vehicle, can pass, where one can move about only by raft. And finally, he predicts to Anu that his sons will die before they have attained the flower of age and that Anu himself will not be qualified to assure the service of the fire altar. The most important matter is saved for later, for the conclusion of the episode: each of these curses leads to an exile to four lands outside the "central" kingdom, which is reserved for the fifth son, the pious son who gives up his youth—Pūru, ancestor of the Pauravas.[37]

> From Yadu are born the Yādavas, from Turvasu the Yavanas, from Druhyu the Bhojas, and from Anu the varieties of Mlecchas.[38]

If the Pauravas' environs are not represented in full by these four peoples—the proper term, since this is a case not just of dynasties but (for at least the second and fourth) of peoples—they certainly provide an adequate sample.[39]

It is difficult, however, to adjust this legend to what the *R̥g Veda* says separately about (1) Yayāti, (2) the "five peoples," and (3) the figures, families, or clans covered by the names of Yadu, Turvaśa (and not -su!), Druhyu, Anu, and Pūru. Strictly speaking, these may be insoluble problems, but they are problems which, as we know from many other examples, are not as important as might be expected.

It has often been emphasized that Yayāti, in the hymns, bears no relation to the "five lands,"[40] This is true. But what do the hymns say about Yayāti? Very little; just enough to substantiate that he was an important and respected figure. Each time he is mentioned, it is as a man of mythical times, notable for his piety: *R̥V* 1,31,17 mentions him beside Manu and Aṅgiras; 1,63,1 puts him on the same level as Vivasvat; he is declared to be the son of Nahuṣa, this last name being sometimes that of a man (8,46,27), sometimes of a clan, of which it is said, moreover, that the fire has been made for its chief as well as for Āyu. That is all. But it is enough to situate Yayāti, in the *R̥g Veda*, at the same point of mythical time that he is given in his appearance in the *Mahābhārata*, and in the same group of venerable "first kings" that the epic regards as his father (Nahuṣa), grandfather (Āyu), and other close ancestors (Vivasvat, Manu). One may thus suppose that he was well known in the time of the redaction of the hymns, already with the rank in which he later appears. To put it simply, the hymns, which are not an encyclopedia, contain no allusions to any legends concerning him, any more than they afford a glimpse of any traditions explaining the origin and occupation of the "five lands." This does not mean that no such legends existed concerning Yayāti and the five peoples or lands. It would be hard to believe that, at the time of the redaction of the hymns, nothing at all could be said about a figure so venerable, or that a more or less concrete origin which could be attributed to notions as precise and commonplace as "the five lands," "the five peoples," was not yet known. Such an *argumentum ex silentio* is here particularly weak, and it could well be that, from Vedic times, Yayāti, through his sons, was regarded as the one who was responsible for the distribution of men among the "Fifths" of the earth, that is, the four cardinal points and the center.

As for a correspondence, if not an equivalence, between the global notion of the "five peoples" and the group of names which designates the sons of Yayāti in the epic, it has been proposed by several critics but rejected by most. There are arguments for both positions.

The main objection, well set forth by Schlerath, is that no passage can be found in the hymns (except 1,108,8) where all five of these names are enumerated—at the most, four appear together—and that these incomplete enumerations are sometimes augmented by other names. The most stable association is between the Turvaśas and the Yadus, but at the time of the "battle of the ten kings," important to the seventh book of the *Ṛg Veda*, the Yadus are missing in the principal hymn (7,18), one strophe of which (16) contains not only the names Turvaśa and Druhyu, but also Yakṣu and Matsya; and, in 7,8,4, it is the Bharatas who are mentioned next to Pūru. Says Schlerath: "In his fundamental study of the families of the authors of the hymns,[41] Hermann Oldenberg has succeeded in verifying a certain connection between Pūru, Yadu, Turvaśa, and Anu, but Druhyu remains apart."

On the other hand, and more important, it seems to me, other texts are cited, like 8,10,5 (addressed to the Twin gods): "May you be in the east or the west, O possessors of high good, may you be among Druhyu, Anu, Turvaśa or Yadu, I call you, come!"[42] The mention of east and west together is evidently equivalent here, in shortened fashion, to the sum of the cardinal points, that is, to the geographical totality of the world (elsewhere indicated by the expression "the five lands"). In such a context, the second enumeration, that of the proper names, could only be a means of saying the same thing from another angle, and expresses, likewise incompletely, the same totality. Thus ethnography reflects topography: humanity (or the arya nationality), analyzed into its typical divisions, fills in the local divisions of the space it occupies.

At the time of the composition of the hymns, was there a direct (father-son) connection between Yayāti and the eponyms of the clans—Yadu and the rest? Let us repeat that Yayāti is scarcely mentioned in the hymnal. It remains likely, above all if one admits that the five ethnic names (Yadu, etc.) recall the "five peoples" and, through them, the five cardinal points (that is, the four plus the center), that the lineage traced back to Yayāti is ancient, and that, existing as early as Vedic times, it was preserved in milieus different from those of the hymnodists and was transmitted into the epic without considerable alteration (the most visible change being the passage from "Turvaśa" to "Turvasu," probably to standardize the final vowel for each of the five names). If, on the other hand, one were to believe that the five proper names (Yadu, etc.) were not originally connected with the five peoples, he would have to admit that they had been introduced later into the Yayāti legend, a supposition that does not bear up well: the legend of Yayāti parceling out the world to his sons conforms to an ancient, Indo-Iranian type, and, accordingly, the sons would at all times have required names. Must it be assumed that the five names we read of were later substitutes for another series of five which had supposedly disappeared in the meantime?

3. The Old and the Young, Yayāti and Aun

The very content of the legend of Yayāti and his sons, as it is set forth in the first book of the *Mahābhārata*, guarantees its great antiquity. If we set aside Yayāti's father-in-law, the sorcerer, and his curse, the action takes place in the following way: a king, crushed by senility, entreats his sons to give him their youth, and one of them accepts, assuring his father of a thousand years of vigor; the king expels from the land the older brothers who have refused, and makes the youngest, who has accepted, his successor. Two well-known and certainly archaic themes are reunited here: the reservoir of vitality which sons constitute for the royal father and which is available to him through a transferral; and the curses and exiles which fall upon those of the father's sons who have maltreated him and the reward bestowed on the one who has behaved devotedly.

As to the first theme, important since it is the one which has allowed or prompted the Yayāti legend to be passed down in the same package as that of Kāvya Uśanas, the reader may recall a famous Scandinavian story, that of Aun or Áni, the king of Uppsala, one of the still legendary members of the Ynglingar dynasty. Here, then, is a resumé, following the *Ynglingasaga* of Snorri Sturluson, chapter 25.[43]

At the age of sixty, king Aun, by sacrificing his oldest son, obtained sixty new years of life and reign from the god Óðinn, who was fond of human sacrifices. Once this reprieve had elapsed, Óðinn informed him that he would continue to live so long as he sacrificed, to Óðinn himself, one of his sons every ten years. Aun sacrificed down to the seventh, whom he survived by ten years, but his legs could no longer support him and he was carried about in a chair. He sacrificed the eighth, and survived ten years longer without leaving his bed. He sacrificed the ninth, and lived ten more years, drinking from a horn like a nursling (*þá drakk hann horn sem lébarn*). Finally, he had only one son left, but the Swedes prevented this one from being sacrificed. "King Aun died and was put under a tumulus at Uppsala (*ok er hann heygðr at Upsölum*). From then on, the act of dying of old age without sickness was called 'sickness of Áni' (*ánasótt*)."

This legend was brilliantly commented upon by Samuel Eitrem,[44] who emphasized the importance of the number nine (or ten, that is to say, "nine full"). What interests us here is that the sacrifice of the sons periodically prolongs the life of the father. And here the sons are not the menacing rivals whom the father must eliminate (in this respect the two stories which Eitrem has compared, that of Aun and his children and that of Ouranos and the Ouranides, must be distinguished from one another); rather, they are the docile, useful instruments in a technique for promoting the longevity of the king, their father.[45]

The story of Yayāti is certainly different on many counts. What the Indian king obtains is no mere prolongation of life, allowing the aging process to continue to take its inexorable toll upon him even during the reprieve, extending itself beyond the usual limit and resulting in a woeful caricature of existence. It is rather a new and durable youth, a millennium of youth. Along with this difference, Yayāti's technique varies from that of Aun. Aun seeks life; he thus takes the life of his sons, or rather offers it in sacrifice to the master of that mechanism, Óðinn. Yayāti seeks youth; he thus takes the youth of one of his sons—the only one who has agreed and consequently counts in this story of exchange, the others not entering in—thanks to the privilege which the master of the mechanism, the sorceror, has given him; and what is required of the obedient son is not death but a temporary decay. Finally, the conclusions are divergent in the extreme: at the end of his repeated trafficking with life and death, Aun, now ruthless and impotent, must take his own turn, dying ten years after he has immolated all but the last of his sons; and even if he had sacrificed his last son, he would necessarily have died ten years later. But between Yayāti and Pūru, the barter of youth for old age comes to a negotiated end, and a reverse exchange returns things to their former state, the donor recovering a youth which appears to have been happily preserved by the very miracle of its transfer, while Yayāti, the recipient, gets back his unaltered old age.

Despite these differences in application, the principle in the two operations is the same, and the fact that Yayāti's aging is accelerated and artificial, while Aun's is natural, changes nothing: psychologically, both kings wish to escape their condition, whether death or old age, and each considers he has the right to do so. Mystically or technically, it is not through a stranger—a prisoner or a slave for example—that either king can receive this additional life or vitality, but solely from his descendants: from one or more of his sons.

4. The Disrespectful Sons and the Partition of the World, Yayāti and Noah

The second theme is none other than the one by which the Book of Genesis (9,18–29) explains the multiplicity and the distribution of the great races which appeared on earth soon after the flood:

The sons of Noah who went forth from the ark were Shem, Ham, and Japheth. Ham was the father of Canaan. These three were the sons of Noah, and from these the whole earth was peopled. Noah was the first tiller of the soil. He planted a vineyard; and he drank of the wine, and became drunk, and lay uncovered in his tent. And Ham, the father of Canaan, saw the nakedness of his father, and told his two brothers outside. Then Shem and Japheth took a garment, laid it upon both their shoulders, and walked backward and covered the nakedness of their father; their faces were turned away, and they did not see their father's nakedness. When Noah awoke from his wine and knew what his youngest son had done to him, he said, "Cursed be Canaan; a slave of slaves shall he be to his brothers." He also said, "Blessed by the Lord my God be Shem; and let Canaan be his slave. God enlarge Japheth, and let him dwell in the tents of Shem;[46] and let Canaan be his slave." After the flood Noah lived three hundred and fifty years. And all the days of Noah were nine hundred and fifty years; and he died.

What is at issue here, as verse 19 says, is the peopling, or rather the repeopling, of the entire earth, at least of as much of the earth as the ancient Hebrews knew of or wished to know of. The succeeding chapters locate the three brothers' descendants in this world: Shem will produce, among others, the chosen people;[47] Japheth's sons will occupy roughly the north and west; and, as for Ham, it seems that there was some variation; at first he appears as the ancestor of the peoples situated to the east of Palestine; later he was associated with the south, the land of the blacks (*Αἰθίοπες*, etc.). The distribution is no more than a topographical one with nothing functional about it,[48] its intent being simply to provide an etiology of Canaan's servitude.

It is interesting to see how Tabarī and, after him, Belᶜami, anxious to combine the Quranic and biblical traditions with the "national tradition" of Iran, have connected the legend of Noah with those of J̌amšīd (Yima) and his murderer Zohāk-Beyurasp (Aži Dahāka, called Baēvar-aspa, "of ten thousand horses"). For it is at this point in Iran's "history" that they have inserted the prophet Noah with his flood and his three sons, making Beyurasp, Jamšīd's murderer, and Zohāk, the man with the serpent heads, into two different figures, the one preceding Noah and perishing in the flood, the other being born much later among the descendants of Noah's "black" son. The moment is well chosen: all told, Noah's three sons beget the black peoples (Ham), the yellow (Japhet), and the white (Shem), that is to say, a close approximation of the humanity which Afrīdūn, the conqueror of Zohāk, will have, or should have, to distribute among his three sons as the subjects of their kingdoms. However, as Afrīdūn comes in direct line from the Iranian tradition, his geography and ethnography are not those of the Bible. Thus, when he makes the "partition of the world," the three portions he distributes will consist of the Byzantines, the Iranians augmented by Hindustan, and the Turanians supplemented by China; to their good fortune or otherwise, the blacks are forgotten. Here, in Belᶜami's account, is the Islamic version of the sin not only of Ham but of two of the three brothers:

Noah lived three hundred more years after the flood. . . . It was from the eighty persons who were saved with Noah that God produced the men whom we see. Now all the world's peoples, the Jews, the Christians, and the Muslims, regard Noah's flood as a veritable fact. There are only the Magi who know neither of Noah nor the flood and who say that, since the world exists, it has always been as it is. . . .

Know then that all creatures, after Noah, have come from Shem, Ham, and Japhet. The Arabs, the Persians, the men of white countenance, the good men, the jurisconsults, the learned and the wise[49] are from the race of Shem, and here is why. One day, Noah was asleep and the wind raised his apparel and exposed his genital parts without his being aware of it. Japhet passed near Noah and saw his genital parts; he burst out laughing and began to jest, and did not replace the covers on him. Ham, Japhet's brother, arrived next; he looked at Noah, burst out laughing and began to jest, and passed by without covering his father. Shem came after his brothers and, seeing Noah in an indecent position, averted his eyes and hid his father's nudity. Noah then awoke and asked Shem what had happened. Having learned that Ham and Japhet had passed near him and that they had laughed, he cursed them, saying: "May God alter the seed of your loins."

After that, all the men and the fruits of the land of Ham became black. The black grape is to be counted among the latter.

The Turks, Slavs, and Gog and Magog, with several other peoples who are unknown to us, descend from Japhet.

Ham and Japhet were thus punished for having laughed while seeing their father's genital parts.[50]

Though it is certainly a vain wish, one would like to know the source from which the authors of Genesis took the theme of the partition of the world, and also the names of the three parties involved. The form which they gave it is in any case closer to the Indian legend (Yayāti and his sons) than to the Iranian (Ferīdūn and his sons), and, like the Indian, it not only brings together in one generation a reflective son and his heedless brothers, but also a son who honors his father and others who disregard him.

So far we have considered only one version of the adventure of Yayāti and his sons: the one which figures in the "Book of Kings" which serves as an overture to the *Mahābhārata*. It is, however, only one variant among others. In the fifth book of the same poem, a noticeably different version is presented in which the agings and the miraculous transferrals of age are eliminated, and the facts are introduced in a manner still closer to the story of Noah and his sons.

In the moving fifth book, in which so many forces in the two camps try to prevent the imminent conflict between the two groups of cousins and, for that end, attempt to obtain from Duryodhana certain concessions—there comes a moment when Duryodhana's own father, Dhṛtarāṣṭra, physically blind, spiritually clear-sighted, but weak of character, explains to his son that he would not be the first prince of the family to see himself passed over in favor of someone else. He cites him several examples: in the not too distant past, among the sons of Pratīpa, it was the second son, their grandsire Śāntanu, who assumed the royalty because his older brother had pursued an unavoidable religious vocation; even in Dhṛtarāṣṭra's own generation, it was not he, the disabled one, but Pāṇḍu, his junior, who became king. But his first reference is to the ancient example of Pūru, and not without an emphatic recital of the initial members of the geneology:

"It is the lord of creatures, Soma, who, in the beginning, was the progenitor of the Kuru race. The fifth in descent from Soma was Yayāti, son of Nahuṣa. Five sons were born to him, eminent among the rājarṣis. The eldest was the lord Yadu of mighty energy, and the youngest was Pūru, from whom our line descends, and who was the son of Śarmiṣṭhā, herself the daughter of Vṛṣaparvan while Yadu, O best of Bharatas, was born of Devayānī and, therefore, was the grandson of Śukra, also called Kāvya, of immeasurable energy. This ancestor of the Yādavas [= Yadu], endowed with strength and honored for his vigor, was filled with pride and, foolishly, despised (*avamene*) the *kṣatra*, the class of warriors. Misguided by pride in his strength, he did not obey the instructions of his father; on the contrary, this invincible prince despised (*avamene*) his father, and also his brothers. On this earth with its four limits, Yadu became powerful and, having subdued the princes, dwelt in the city named after the elephant [= Hastināpura, which will later become the capital of Pāṇḍu and, after their victory, of the Pāṇḍavas].[51] His father Yayāti, son of Nahuṣa, at the peak of anger, cursed this son. O son of Gāṅdhārī, and expelled him from the kingdom.[52] Moreover, those brothers who fell in with Yadu, proud of his strength, the angered Yayāti cursed them, his sons, as well.[53] Then that excellent prince installed his youngest son on the throne, Pūru, the son who had met his wish.[54] Thus even the eldest may be deprived of the royal dignity while the youngest obtains it by the filial respect which he shows to the aged (*vṛddhopasevayā*)."[55]

As can be seen, this text from the fifth book presents only one of the two themes which were joined together in the first; the fault of the sons, with the exception of Pūru, is their failure to act in conformity with their father's wishes. They "despise" him, Yadu through pride in his own strength, the three other older brothers by being too susceptible to their elder's prestige. In contrast, Pūru's merit is in respecting and listening to his father. There is, of course, no reason to claim a unity for the two variants, or to place them in any chronological perspective.[56] Their coexistence proves that the legend of Yayāti and Pūru was widespread enough to be told in diverse, but equivalent, ways. It also shows that the essential element was not this or that particular or picturesque detail concerning the lack of respect toward the father, but the very fact of this want of respect.

As to the conclusion—that is, the distribution of the parts of the earth between the brothers—the short passage in the fifth book says nothing about it and specifies no other lands for Yayāti to consign to his first four sons. Still, there was no call for it either, since the only important thing for Dhṛtarāṣṭra's argument is that Yadu be deprived and Pūru be gratified with the throne in that unique part of the earth which interests Duryodhana, the "central land" of which Hastināpura is the capital. For Yadu, at least, the curse (*śaśāpa*) is expressively and immediately followed by his expulsion from the kingdom (*rājyāc ca vyapāropayat*): he had to go somewhere, and it is natural, despite the text's brevity, to suppose that, under the same conditions, similar curses (*śaśāpa*) would have been leveled against the three other sons as well. In contrast, the variant of the first book, recounting the story on its own terms for itself, and not for the purpose of making a point in some political argument, was the natural place to name the allocated lands. This, in fact, is what we find. But the most important formula was saved for later, making its appearance not in the first episode of Yayāti's adventure but in the second, which we will examine now. Let us bear in mind the formula that Yayāti will use in this second episode to sum up, for his interlocutor Indra, the decisions he has made with respect to his sons and what he has said to Pūru:

> gaṅgāyamunayor madhye kr̥tsno 'yaṃ viṣayas tava
> madhye pr̥thivyās tvaṃ rājā bhrātaro 'ntyādhipās tava.

The whole land between the Ganges and the Yamunā is yours: you, yourself, will be king over *the center* of the earth; your brothers will be lords of *the outlying regions*.[57]

2

YAYĀTI AND HIS DAUGHTER'S SONS

1. Yayāti's Four Grandsons and the Three Functions

The scene shifts, and so do the dramatis personae except for Yayāti, who keeps the leading role. In fact, this is not a second act but another play, whose plot does not exactly tie in with that of the first. As the curtain rises, Yayāti has finished aging, and his troublesome wife, the sorcerer's daughter, makes no further appearance, not even in retrospect. Only two sons are known to him, his successor Pūru and Yadu, who appear twice, mere supernumeraries, mentioned in that order and, it would seem, on good terms with each other. Moreover, Yayāti has a devoted daughter, Mādhavī, whose mother is unnamed, and by her he is the grandfather of four excellent youths who are already kings. In short, positively or negatively, everything seems to have been set up for an idyllic finale.

Actually, his daughter's four sons have had curious births. The fifth book of the *Mahābhārata* describes them in a charming account which will have to occupy us later,[1] since it constitutes another episode, another drama—an intermediary one—in a life which accordingly seems to unfold in a trilogy the titles of which could be "The Father and the Sons," "The Father and the Daughter," and "The Father and the Grandsons." The first book of the *Mahābhārata* has retained, without good transitions, only the sons and the grandsons, while the fifth book, neglecting the sons, makes the third drama the harmonious sequel to the second.

Having become old once and for all, Yayāti leaves the kingdom to his heir Pūru in order to observe that precious interval between life and death which we call retirement and which is, in the Indian sense of the word, a retreat, a long period in the forest in the company of hermit saints. There, with a profusion of new merits, he perfects those which he has earned in his exemplary reign as "universal sovereign," a title which the poem readily confers upon him. As a result, he ascends to heaven at his death without difficulty.

As for his grandsons, whom he does not seem to have known very well, they live and prosper in kingdoms which are not all those of their respective fathers. They, too, are accumulating merits, but merits differentiated according to four highly interesting definitions applied to them formerly by another sage, Gālava, when he was addressing their mother Mādhavī after watching over their births:

jāto dānapatiḥ putras tvayā śūras tathā 'paraḥ
satyadharmaratas cānyo yajvā cāpi tathā paraḥ

To you is born a son who is a lord of gifts, a second who is a hero, another who is devoted to justice and truth, and yet another, a sacrificer.[2]

The "lord of gifts," that is, the lord of alms, is in essence something else; or rather the alms are only the good use which he makes of that which constitutes his real nature: he is prodigiously rich. Containing the term *vasu*, "material goods," in his name, he is in fact called *Vasumanas*.[3] At the moment of his arrival in the world, the poet of the fifth book has introduced him clearly:[4]

tato vasumanā nāma vasubhyo vasumattaraḥ
vasuprabho narapatiḥ sa babhūva vasupradaḥ

Named Vasumanas, richer than the rich, equal to the Vasu (the Rich) themselves, he became a king who was a giver of riches.[4]

Thus, in the order of their births—which is also the ascending order of the functions—these four figures are characterized by their excellence: one in the third function (*vasu*, riches), one in the second (*śūra*, hero), and two in two aspects of the first: one moral, a total devotion to truth (*satya*) and virtue (*dharma*), the other religious or, more precisely liturgical, an assiduous observance of sacrifices (*yajña*).

These four on the earth, and their grandfather in heaven, do not foresee the occasion of what is perhaps to be their first encounter.

2. Yayāti's Sin, Fall and Redemption, and the Transfer of Merits

On the strength of what seem to be inexhaustible merits, Yayāti lives for millions of years in celestial comfort, highly esteemed by the various divine groups that one encounters in heaven. He even tours the numerous paradises, sojourning sometimes in one, sometimes in another. But one day a fault appears in his perfection: in the fifth book, this takes place mentally and spontaneously, while in book one it takes place verbally and under provocation. The fifth book's rendition is especially moving.[5]

After these innumerable millennia spent in the greatest happiness, one day, seated amid the most illustrious ṛṣis, he is overcome by a foolish sense of pride which produces a feeling of scorn for the gods, ṛṣis, and men. Indra, who is present, reads his heart. Less insightful, the ṛṣis experience this mental catastrophe without understanding it: up to this instant they have felt no uneasiness in treating him as an old friend and colleague, but suddenly they no longer recognize him. They see him as a stranger, an intruder. The air is filled with confused questions: "Who is he? Son of what king? Why is he in heaven? What acts have earned him this reward? Where has he carried out his time of asceticism? What is known of him? Who knows him?" And the whole household of heaven, the charioteers, the gatekeepers, all answer: "We do not know him." King Yayāti, in fact, has changed. By his sin, he has lost his splendor. And if only that were all he had lost!

In the account in the first book, he strikes us as more rash than guilty.[6] One day he pays a visit to Indra and, in the course of a free and open exchange, the king of the gods amiably asks him some questions: "What did you say to your son Pūru when he took on himself your decrepitude and when you gave him the kingdom?" This is the moment when Yayāti gives him the answer—a good answer—cited above: "I said to him: 'The whole land between the Ganges and the Yamunā is yours: you, yourself, will be king over the middle of the earth; your brothers will be princes over the outlying regions.' In addition I said to him . . ."[7] And then, in thirteen distichs, Yayāti recounts the excellent moral counsel, wholly unoriginal, which he gave to Pūru on that occasion. The god then asks a second question, and Yayāti fails to see the danger, the trap. "King Yayāti, son of Nahuṣa, having fulfilled all your duties, you left your palace and went into the forest. I ask you: to whom are you equal in ascetic merits?" The answer comes: "Neither among men, nor among the gods, the Gandharvas, nor the maharṣis, am I able, O Indra, to cite anyone who is my equal in ascetic merits!" Immediately the god's verdict is pronounced: "Because you scorn your superiors, your equals, your inferiors, your merits will vanish and you must fall from heaven!"

Mental or verbal, such is indeed the outcome of this burst of vanity. The author of the fifth book shows the king trembling with fear, burning with remorse under his faded garlands, shorn of his crown, ornaments, and robes. He falls, a puppet without strings, amid the mockery of the celestial host. And soon the celestial bouncer charged with handling such eviction notices appears beside him and confirms that there is no longer a place for him among the gods.[8]

The hapless king does, however, keep enough presence of mind to concern himself with where he should land on earth. In the first book, right after being condemned and before his fall, he says to Indra: "King of the gods, if truly my disregard of men, of the Gandharvas, of the ṛṣis, of the gods, has made me lose the (celestial) worlds, deprived as I am of the world of the gods, allow me to fall into the midst of good men (*satāṃ madhye*)!"[9] This the god readily accords him, imposing no conditions. In the fifth book, Yayāti appears to be endowed, during his descent, with the power to affect his own course: like an astronaut, able to determine, with his jets and parachutes, the place of his splashdown, he reflects: "If I must fall, let me at least fall among the good!"—and, setting his course by the odor of a column of smoke that rises from an enormous sacrifice, he directs his fall toward the place where the men, as he is able to predict with evident accuracy, are pious.[10]

Now this sacrifice—a *vājapeya*, one of the sacrifices proper to royalty—is being offered by four kings conjointly, a strange and unusual thing. And these kings are none other than Yayāti's own four grandsons who, over and beyond their characteristic specialities—Vasumanas' riches and generosity, Pratardana's prowess, Śibi's veracity, and Aṣṭaka's assiduous practice of sacrifices—have in common the highest degree of morality which, to tell the truth, more or less blurs their functional colorations and tends to reduce them all to the generalized type of the perfect king. From the logs of their *āhavanīya*, their "libation fire," the smoke rises, in accord with the best Vedic tradition, as a path connecting heaven and earth—a shifting pathway, or rather a river which the poet compares to the Ganges in its celebrated descent.[11]

Does Yayāti's fall, bringing him into their midst, take him down to the ground? Not according to the first book:[12] it is while seeing him fall, still far off in the sky, that Aṣṭaka engages Yayāti in a long dialogue, first begging pardon for being so impolite as to ask him who he is; and it seems that the conversation is next generalized to take in all four terrestrial observers well before this space module is ready to land. But the answer is yes if we accept the first words which the fifth book devotes to this occasion.[13] Here it is on earth that the four kings interrogate him: "Who are you? Of what race, of what country, of what city? Are you a Yakṣa, a god, a Gandharva, a Rākṣasa? You do not seem to be a human being. What is your intention?" He answers with precision, summing up his misfortune with the most unexpected brevity: "I am Yayāti, the rājarṣi Yayāti. Through the exhaustion of my merit, I have fallen from heaven. I desired to fall among good men: I have fallen among you. . . ." But a little further on, when this happy family gathering has ended, it is said that "the king rose again without touching the surface of the earth," *samāruroha nṛpatiḥ aspṛśan vasudhātalam*,[14] and, in a detailed repetition of the narrative—a new, slightly different variant—which follows this ending, the fact is confirmed: he did not touch the earth, *na pṛthvīm aspṛśat padā*.[15]

This point is a secondary one. The important thing is the conclusion itself with the series of discourses, the competing generous offers which lead up to it. The variants agree on the following: the four kings offer to transfer their merits to Yayāti so that he may regain his place among the gods, but Yayāti refuses, saying that only brahmans have the right to receive alms, sometimes adding that he would not want to deprive them of their own blessings. But the details differ from text to text.

In the first book each king in turn—Aṣṭaka, Pratardana, Vasumanas, and Śibi, in that order—says nearly the same thing to the omniscient Yayāti, and this in a form that resembles a celebrated

Avestan *gāthā*: "I ask you—do not fall!—do I possess any worlds, *lokāḥ*, in heaven or in the atmosphere; if I possess any, they are yours."[16] The mechanism of merits and rewards is thus interpreted in the manner of acquiring real estate, as the acquisition of bigger or smaller lots in the celestial expanses. And each hears the answer that his extraordinary merits have indeed entitled him to possess immense worlds at the three levels of the universe, although their various merits are not specified and do not appear to be appreciably different from one king to the next. But Yayāti obstinately refuses to accept a gift, or even to purchase these domains by the symbolic payment of a blade of grass. Such is the deadlock, all the more serious since the kings point out, through their spokesman Aṣṭaka, that they will be unable to take back the merits they have surrendered and that if Yayāti persists in his refusal, they will accompany him to his final destination, the "terrestrial" (*bhauma*) hell.[17] The way out is provided not by a *deus ex machina* but by a number of *vehicula de caelo*: Aṣṭaka suddenly sees five golden chariots appear in the air. "Whose are these chariots?" he asks Yayāti, who answers: "These chariots will carry you to the celestial regions." But there are five chariots, not four, and the four kings have no difficulty in convincing him to ascend to heaven in the one which is plainly not for them.[18] And so, counterbalanced by the abnegation of the "four kings of today," atonement is made for that moment of pride which had just deprived "yesterday's king" of the merits gained over thousands of years. And at the same stroke, the abnegation of the four young kings is rewarded by the promotion which is the final goal of every virtuous life: the celestial ascent. All that remains for them is to get to know each other better while the chariots carry them through space—and at this point we discover that Yayāti, from the outset, had known more than he had allowed to appear.

Impelled by curiosity, Aṣṭaka asked his grandfather, equal to Indra:

"I ask you, O king, tell me truly: where do you come from, who are you, and whose son? For what you have done, none other than you, neither kṣatriya nor brahman, could have done!"

He answered:

"I am Yayāti, son of Nahuṣa, father of Pūru. In this world I was a 'universal king.' It is to men of my own blood that I disclose my secret: you have before you your mother's father. After having conquered the entire earth, I gave handsome horses to the brahmans for sacrifices: thus the gods enjoy their shares; I gave this entire earth to the brahmans, full of draught animals, with its cows, its gold, its treasures—and there were millions and millions of cows there! It is by truth that heaven and earth are mine, that fire burns among men."[19]

This kind of pride, of self-praise, which disparages no one, is presumably permitted by the gods. Yayāti does not fall again.

In the fifth book, in its first variant, there are not four dialogues: the four kings offer their merits together to their unexpected visitor, and in a very general form: we offer to you "the fruit of our sacrifices and our justice" (*sarveṣāṃ naḥ kratuphalaṃ dharmaśca*). To all four collectively, Yayāti then explains his refusal: "I am not a brahman, I should therefore not accept alms."[20] Here a real *deus ex machina* appears—Yayāti's daughter, the mother of the four kings, who comes out of the woods where she lives in a very special sort of asceticism. The kings recognize her, bow, and ask her the cause of her appearance. She first falls prostrate before her father, then makes the introductions, and finally increases the four kings' deposit by adding to it half of her own merits. A final reinforcement then happens by: the brahman who had been responsible for the birth of the four kings also emerges from the woods and offers an eighth part of the merits acquired by his austerities.[21] This *momentum* is enough to overcome the beneficiary's scruples: full of joy and without having touched the earth, he reascends to the sky, recovering on his way the ornaments and garlands he has lost.[22]

The second variant, which immediately follows the first with no care for composition, is more detailed and puts the functional nature of each of the donors in a clear light. To simplify, the "rich" is marked definitively by the pious use he makes of his riches, and he is characterized not as one who is wealthy per se, but as the distributor of abundant alms. This is a natural circumlocution since it is a matter of announcing merits: in contrast to prowess, veracity, and ritual exactitude, all of which are good in themselves, wealth is a mere raw material, itself neutral, upon which only good usage can confer moral value.

The first to offer his merits is, in fact, Vasumanas, "celebrated in the world as a master of gifts":

> "All that I have obtained in the world by my faultless conduct toward men of all classes, I give to you, that it may be your property! This merit produced by giving, as well as that from patience [*tat phalaṃ dānaśīlasya kṣamāśīlasya tat phalam*], and generally all the merits I have acquired, let them be your property!"[23]

Pratardana is next:

> "Ever devoted to duty, ever ardent for combat [*yuddha-*], that glory proper to warrior lineages (*kṣātravaṃśa-*), which I have obtained in the world, the merit which is attached to the word hero [*vīraśabdaphalam*], let it be your property!"[24]

Then Śibi comes forth:

> "Neither among children nor among women, neither in jest nor in combats, difficulties, calamities, nor dice have I, in the past, uttered a lie [*anr̥taṃ noktapūrvaṃ me*]: by that truth, ascend to heaven! My life, my kingdom, O King, my comforts, I will all abandon, but not truth: by that truth, ascend to heaven! That truth by which I have gratified Dharma and Agni and Indra, by that truth, ascend to heaven [*tena satyena khaṃ vraja*]!"[25]

And finally Aṣṭaka, the sacrificer par excellence:

> "I have offered *puṇḍarīka*, *gosava*, and *vājapeya* sacrifices by the hundreds [*śataśaḥ . . . me caritāḥ . . . kratavaḥ*]: take the merit from these! Jewels, riches, precious robes, I have spared nothing [*me . . . anupayuktāni*] as the cost of my sacrifices: by this truth, ascend to heaven!"[26]

Despite the slight irregularity in the last half-verse, which is borrowed from Śibi's declaration and extends to Aṣṭaka, against our expectation, the type of merit (truthfulness) appropriate to Śibi, despite also the inevitable channeling of Vasumanas' riches into almsgiving, the distinctions are clear: the four grandsons place at their fallen grandfather's disposal a complete set of merits—complete, moreover, according to its trifunctional composition. The first function, the most elevated in dignity, is divided, represented by two of its aspects: truth, which constitutes the basis for morality; and religion, summed up in the superabundant practice of sacrifices. Before we proceed, we should mention that this division is not of the kind usually found in Indian thought: one would sooner expect to find asceticism set against liturgical exactitude, or a religious life of the disquieting type associated with Varuṇa set against the reassuring type of Mitra. Perhaps this exaltation of *satya*, "truth, a life without falsehood," requires an explanation which, at this point in our study, we are not prepared to give. But this open problem does not obscure the trifunctional schema, since a life without falsehood and the performance of rites both enhance the first function. Moreover, the authors of the *Mahābhārata* or, before them, the authors of the legend which has been inserted into the poem, have offered their reflection on this bipartition. The variant in the first book does not end when the five men set off in their celestial chariots. While they are hastening in close formation to the heights of heaven, one of the chariots breaks into the lead, and we can anticipate that it will be one of the two chariots of the first function. And so it is. But which? It is that of Śibi, the veracious grandson, not that of Aṣṭaka, the sacrificer. The latter is astonished, and naïvely he consults the wise old man in the neighboring chariot whom he has just helped to save and whom he does not yet know to be his grandfather.

> "I think that it is I who should go first and that, in all things, Indra is my ally. . . . How is it that Śibi, the son of Uśīnara, and he alone, has, at full speed, left our chariots behind?"[27]

Yayāti answers:

> "Śibi, the son of Uśīnara, in order to go among the gods, has given all that he possessed: that is why he is the foremost among us. Almsgiving, austerity, truthfulness, the observance of duty, modesty, prosperity, patience, amiability, endurance, all this belongs to the incomparable and good king Śibi."[28]

Here again, a slight irregularity shows through: Śibi's "truthfulness," which distinguishes his special glory, is all but submerged in a list of qualities and virtues, making Yayāti's answer inadequate to describe the circumstances. But the fact remains: the old narrative put the representative of the merits gained by veracity above all the rest.

To summarize the points that bear further scrutiny, let us emphasize that Yayāti himself had been carried to heaven and, until his outburst of pride, had been maintained there by a catalogue of merits and benefits as complete as the one which is reconstituted to him by his grandsons' gifts. Indeed, we know from other narratives that he had been prodigiously rich: we will soon see that this is the point of departure for the Mādhavī episode,[29] a further demonstration that, as with Vasumanas, this advantage of his was morally legitimated by the transformation of wealth into alms. To this fundamental fact is added the reckoning which he himself makes at the end of the account in the first book, when Aṣṭaka asks his identity. These *ślokas* have already been quoted.[30] They enumerate three items, the last two only slightly diluted: (1) I have conquered the entire earth; (2) I have given to brahmans countless gifts (as *dakṣiṇās*) and also the raw materials, the animals, for their sacrificial activities; (3) I have been and am truthful. He has thus, during his terrestrial life, himself combined—in addition to riches and generosity like those of Vasumanas—the various characteristics which are to be distributed in the subsequent generation among: (1) the warrior Pratardana; (2) the sacrificer Aṣṭaka; (3) the veracious Śibi. And Yayāti, too, concludes this description of himself by exalting his "truth," that is truthfulness, above all:

"It is by truth that heaven and earth are mine, by my truth that fire burns among men. Never have I spoken a word that was vain, for the good give homage to the truth.[31] It is by their truth that all the gods, the munis, the worlds are worthy of honor, such is my deep conviction."[32]

The meaning of the story that ends with these words is clear, and can be summarized briefly. Having amassed a great store of his own personal merits, reckoned according to the three functions—by distributed wealth, by conquests, by sacrificing and always telling the truth—king Yayāti ascends to heaven after death and gains his own celestial seat. After a long stay there, a prideful thought comes to him, whether spontaneously or under provocation, which destroys his mystical resources at one stroke and makes him fall toward the earth, with the "terrestrial hell" as his final destination. But his four grandsons, each of whom excels in only one of the kinds of meritorious activity which have combined in Yayāti's life to form a natural synthesis, place their partial treasures conjointly at his disposal and reconstitute for him, under the same diversified headings, a complete set of merits able to transform his fall into an ascent and restore him to his place in heaven.

3. Yima's Sin, Disgrace, and Heritage

This plot, touching in all its strangeness, which one would willingly hold up as an example to the grandsons of today, immediately brings to mind the tragic end of the most illustrious of all the "first kings" of Iranian legend, Yima Xšaēta, Yima "the King par excellence," or as the epic calls him, J̌amšīd.[33] As we have seen,[34] this highly complex figure meets his exact Indian homonym, Yama, at only a few points, the latter, since the *R̥g Veda*, being almost a god and, in the subsequent literature, a god no different from others, save that his field is exclusively the world of the dead. At all levels of the Iranian tradition, the main features of the legend of Yima follow a course that shows no correspondence with the theology of Yama. I give here only a rough outline:

For a long time Yima holds the "sovereign empire over all the lands," and his reign, of untold prosperity, is protected by the *x*^{v}*arənah*, that mark of divine election which guarantees and expresses the legitimacy of a king.[35] But one day he commits a sin. According to the single passage that mentions it in the remaining post-gāthic *Avesta*, the sin is lying: his extraordinary prosperity, *Yašt* 19,33 says emphatically, lasted until "he lied," until he "began to think the lying word, contrary to truth."[36] The subsequent literature has given the fault a different orientation. According to the *Dātastān i Denīk*, 36,16, it was a matter of ambition: he was "deceived by the demon and thus rendered full of zeal for the supreme sovereignty and not for the service of Ohrmazd."[37] But according to all the texts from Muslim times, with certain specifications and diverse settings—some quite picturesque—it is simply pride, a pride sometimes inspired and fanned by the demon. Some Zoroastrian texts supply in addition a description of the origin of the sin of pride. For example, the Parsee *Rivāyat*, published by Spiegel and translated by Christensen, tells the story as follows:

> When seventy years had passed, it befell that Satan [Ahriman] got free, and, when he came before King J̌amšīd, he succeeded by one means and another in driving out the reason from his body. On this occasion he exerted his enmity upon J̌amšīd in such a way as to make him very prideful and egotistical. J̌amšīd called together all the grandees of the different *kišvars*—all the dasturs, mobads, and lords—and spoke in these terms to the mobads

and grandees: "I am the sovereign of the entire earth. What God is there beside me? The earth's creatures live through me, I am the God of all men." When the aged dignitaries heard this speech, they remained confused, bent their heads, and no one understood the meaning of his speech. But when the words had been pronounced, the divine Glory abandoned him.[38]

In Ferdowsi, J̌amšīd's declaration is in the same style:

All men were obedient to the king's command and the world was pervaded by the pleasant sounds of music. And so years went by until the royal farr [= *x*ᵛ*arənah*] was wrested from him. The reason for it was that the king, who had always paid homage to God, now became filled with vanity and turned away from him in forgetfulness of the gratitude he owed him. He summoned those of his followers who were held in highest esteem and in these words addressed his nobles of long experience: "I recognize no lord but myself. It was through me that skills appeared on earth, and no throne however famed has ever beheld a monarch like me. It was I who adorned the world with beauty and it is by my will that the earth has become what it now is. Sunshine, sleep, and repose all come through me, and even your clothing and what enters your mouths originate from me. Power, crown, and kingship are my prerogative. Who can claim that anyone but I am king? By means of drugs and other medicaments the world has been brought to such a level of health that sickness and death befall no one. Who but I have banished death from amongst mankind, although many kings have been upon the earth? It is because of me that you have minds and souls in your bodies. And now that you are aware that all this was accomplished by me, it is your duty to entitle me 'Creator of the World.'"[39] The priests [mobads] to a man remained with heads bowed low, none daring to ask "Why?" or "How?" But as soon as he had made his speech, the farr departed from him.[40]

More soberly, al Thaᶜālibī says the same thing:

Possessing in abundance the goods of the world, and also immense power and prestige, when J̌im had arrived at the apogee of his power, and when his reign and his life prolonged themselves, then his heart hardened, he became haughty and presumptuous, full of pride and arrogance, lofty and imperious, and he said: "I am your supreme lord." He refused to render homage to God and came thereby to attribute divinity to himself. Then his flame was not long to extinguish itself.[41]

This "flame" is an attenuated interpretation of the *x*ᵛ*arənah*, that "Glory" which had been borne with prestige by the Avestan Yima.

But here a most remarkable theme appears in the Zoroastrian literature, still having very much to do with the nature of the x^{v}*arənah*. Two texts have been conserved, diverging on some details, agreeing on others and in their total structure. One is *Yašt* 19,34–38, taken here, scarcely retouched, from Christensen's translation:

> But when he began to think of the lying word, contrary to the truth [*draogəm vāčim aṅhaiθīm*], the x^{v}*arənah* removed itself from him, visibly, in the form of a bird. Seeing the x^{v}*arənah* take flight, Yima Xšaēta of the good herds began to wander sadly and, succumbing to enmities, he remained hidden under the earth.
>
> The first x^{v}*arənah* [*paoirīm̄* x^{v}*arənō*] took flight, the x^{v}*arənah* took flight from Yima Xšaēta, the x^{v}*arənah* left Yima, son of Vīvaṅhat, in the form of the bird Vārəǧna. This x^{v}*arənah* Miθra seized, he of vast pasture grounds, of fine hearing, of a thousand talents. We sacrifice to Mitra, master of all the lands [*dahyunam daṅhupaitim*], whom Ahura Mazdā has created the most endowed with x^{v}*arənah* [x^{v}*arənaṅuhastəməm*] among the spiritual Yazatas.
>
> When the second x^{v}*rənah* [*bitīm* x^{v}*arənō*] took flight, when the x^{v}*arənah* took flight from Yima Xšaēta, when the x^{v}*arənah* left Yima, son of Vīvaṅhat, in the form of the bird Vārəǧna, Θraētaona, the descendant of the house of the Āθwya, of the powerful house, seized it, so that he became the most victorious of victorious men [*vərəθravanąm vərəθravastəmō*], beside Zaraθuštra; he who conquered the three-mouthed, three-headed, six-eyed, thousand-talented, very strong Aži Dahāka, the demonic *druǰ*, the malefactor against the living, the villain whom Aṅra Mainyu had created as the most powerful *druǰ* against the bodily world to bring the world of the Aša to death.
>
> When the third x^{v}*arənah* [*θritīm* x^{v}*arənō*] took flight, when the x^{v}*arənah* took flight from Yima Xšaēta, when the x^{v}*arənah* left Yima, son of Vīvaṅhat, in the form of the bird Vārəǧna, Kərəsāspa the courageous seized it, so that he became the strongest of strong men [*mašyanąm uǧrānąm aoǰištō*], excepting Zaraθuštra, by his manly valor [*nairyayāṯ*].[42]

Long considered as the sole witness to the tradition, this account was given various explanations. Even then, the most plausible was that of James Darmesteter which, basing itself on the relationship between the x^{v}*arənah* and fire[43] and on the theory of the three fires—those of the priests, the warriors, and the tiller-breeders—proposed the view that the three x^{v}*arənahs*, which he claimed were fundamentally identical with the fires, leave Yima successively and that these x^{v}*arənas* are respectively those of the first function (the one taken by Miθra), the third (Θraētaona's) and the second (Kərəsāspa's).[44] Christensen objected that, "if it is understandable that the fire of the priests would be received by the god Miθra and that of the warriors by the hero Kərəsāspa, it is less easy to understand why Θraētaona, who was Yima's avenger and the *x*ᵛ*arənah*'s true heir, would have contented himself with the fire of the husbandmen."[45] Darmesteter had foreseen the objection and had gathered the arguments which made this attribution less singular. Notably, he had remarked that "the family of the Āθwya (that of Θraētaona) seems to have been before all else a family of agriculturalists, for the greater part of its members have names composed with the name of the ox."[46] At a later time, the difficulty was surmounted by a Zoroastrian document which Christensen had not taken into account.[47] Another variant of the tripartition of Yima's Glory, more homogeneous and in many respects more satisfying, having its origin in a lost part of the compilation of the *Avesta*, is found conserved in the *Dēnkart* (VII,I,25–27,32,36–37), and this time the text itself gives clear expression to the trifunctional interpretation.

25–27. In another epoch, it [= the "Word"] returned, from the share allotted by the distribution [*baxšišn*] of Yam's *xvarrah* to the religious function of agriculture [*vastryōšīh*], to Frētōn of the family of the Aswyān, still in his mother's womb; and thereby he became victorious [*pērōʒkarīhast*]. . . . By agriculture, the third religious function [*dēn sitīkar pēšak*], he taught men the medicine of the body (*tanbiʒiškīh*) which makes it possible to disclose the plague and chase away sickness. And he performed numerous wonders and actions beneficial to the world. . . .

32. In another epoch, it returned to Sāmān Karsāsp, from the share allotted by the distribution of Yam's *xvarrah* to the warrior estate [*artēštārīh*], the second religious function [*ditīkar dēn pēšak*]. Thanks to it, he was able to kill the Horned Dragon which swallowed horses and men, the *dēv* Gandarw of golden heels, as well as several other demons created by the *dēv* and the *druǰ* ravaging creation. . . .

36–37. In the same epoch [= under the reign of King Kai Ūs], it returned to Ōšnar, still in the womb of his mother, he who was very wise [*pur-ʒēr*] thanks to the *xvarrah* of Yam [thanks, evidently, to the last available portion of this *xvarrah*, corresponding to the first function]. Speaking in his mother's womb, he taught her several wonders. At his birth, he struck the Evil Spirit and refuted the assertions of the *mar* Fračya, the worshiper of the *dēv*. He became minister for Kai Ūs and, under his reign, administered the seven continents. He discovered [taught] the art of regulating speech and several other sciences useful to men; and the non-aryans were conquered in debate. He lavished the most sage counsels [*hu-frahaxt-tom*] in the aryan lands.[48]

Thus what was once, before his sin, a "totality" comprised of the unification of three elements necessary for royal success, now, after his sin, splits up into three shares each defined by one of the three functions (agriculture, martial force, sagacity and religion). And each of these functions transports itself (awaiting, it seems, a new synthesis constituting the "*x*ᵛ*arənah* of the Kavis") onto a great man about to be born, who is characterized by his excellence in the corresponding function: the first will be a healer (who, at this point in the tradition, is not yet a king); the second, a sort of Heracles; and the third, the wise minister, miracle worker, and administrator of justice for a mythical king. Darmesteter's intuition has thus been confirmed.[49]

Provided with this element of comparison, we should return to Yayāti to observe that, if the legend of his burst of pride and his punishment by the total loss of his merits is of the same value and the same direction as Yima's sin and the flight of the thirds of the *x*ᵛ*arənah*, then the conclusion moves at once in a parallel and in an opposite direction: optimistic and idyllic just as the story of Yima is dramatic and pessimistic.

Yayāti's loss of the merits which he acquired on earth in the three functional spheres—the highest having two aspects—is not a flight but an irremediable destruction. There is no one, neither a better nor a younger person, who can inherit or win them: they have been consumed in the flash of an evil thought; they no longer exist. As compensation, Yayāti has what Yima does not have: four devoted grandsons as meritorious as he, with the reservation that each has invested his most essential merits in the area covered by a single function or functional fragment, thus making it necessary that the four partial treasures be added together in order to reconstitute the full treasure which the grandfather so suddenly lost. Moreover, these four grandsons are united closely not only at heart. On the day of his misfortune, they find themselves physically reunited on a common sacrificial terrain, all offering the same sacrifice: the synthesis Yayāti needs is thus completely ready for him, prefigured in their unity of purpose. The synthesis is offered to him, and, after a flood of niceties, it is accepted: Yayāti is saved and returned to his place in heaven without, it would seem, actually having to dispossess his grandsons, whose heroic donations have, in turn, presumably yielded them further merits equally capable of assuring them of heaven. If we were to reduce matters to a brief formula, we could say: Yima, by lying or by pride, witnesses the flight of his total Glory, which becomes divided, in accordance with the three functions, into three portions, which later pass on to three figures who will thereby in the future each become eminent in the function which corresponds to his respective portion, leaving Yima himself lost and without refuge; Yayāti, by his pride, witnesses the destruction of the full sum of his merits, which soon afterward is reconstituted for him by the addition of merits which four younger figures, each eminent in one of the functions or a fraction thereof, transfer to him—jointly and voluntarily—thus restoring his former glory to him. In the Iranian case we have division and dispersion; in the other, reconciliation and fusion. The beneficiary in India is homologous to the one who is stripped in Iran, and the recipients in Iran are homologous to the givers in India. But the lines of movement are the same, though traveled in opposite directions, and the structure of the transferred material, whether by loss, with differentiation, or by gift, with synthesis, is identical in both cases. The resemblance and the inversion are especially evident in the decisive scene of each drama: it is before the gathered dignitaries—the four functional classes which he has just founded—that the Iranian J̌amšīd makes the boastful declaration that disperses and expels the functional component parts of his Glory from him;[50] it is before his gathered grandsons—specialists in the four functional merits—that Yayāti confesses his sin of pride, in consequence of which the four types of merits, added together, are transferred to him.

Similarity and inversion are probably explained, at least partially, by the nature of what may here be called the stake. The *x*ᵛ*arənah* is a "free gift" of God, which could well be *lost* by the man on whom God had conferred it, but which could be *won* by no man. Moreover, it could not be *destroyed* by any man's sin, but only *withdrawn* by God and transferred by him onto other men. The Indian drama, on the other hand, is developed around the merits of man, around the *phala*, "fruit," of actions. This fruit may evidently be *destroyed* by the sin of a man who, without the gods' intervention, has *won* it; but it may also be reconstituted by a new human effort—by the same man if he is still alive, or by others. It is thus that Yayāti's grandsons reestablish their grandfather in his celestial beatitude by turning to his account the merits which they have won themselves.

4. The Truth

Once the general parallelism between the Indian and the Iranian accounts has been observed, a trait of the former calls for further examination. Up to now, we have admitted that the four types of merits possessed by Yayāti's grandsons, like the four sources of his own merits during his terrestrial reign, were homogeneous, the merits of the first function merely being considered under two aspects. We have noted, however, that the principle of this bipartition was not the one encountered in other, quite frequent bipartitions of this function. Rigorousness in cultic matters is balanced here by the practice of a social virtue.[51]

But what is this virtue? It is the truth, *satya*, that is, respect for the truth and, very strictly, according to Śibi's own words, an existence in which no lie, whether small or large, with or without extenuating circumstances, is ever uttered. And this is the virtue which, repeatedly and emphatically, is given primacy over all the other sources of merits—riches expended in gifts and alms, the exercise of valor, and the multiplication of sacrifices. In one case the specialist in this virtue, Śibi, wins the race to paradise in which Aṣṭaka, the sacrificer, naïvely believes himself deserving of the best place.[52] In the other, Yayāti, by his analytic description of his own merits, saves *satya* for last, raising the tone of the whole speech, attributing to himself, through his respect for *satya*, a creator's role, a cosmic power.[53] The suspicion thus arises that this fourth source of merits, which complicates the distribution of the whole over the three functions and risks upsetting their structure, is not of the same nature as the three others but dominates or conditions them. What we have before us, then, may be the merits of the three functions and, above them, the more important merits of veracity, the absence of lying.

Even if we hold to the uniform interpretation that keeps the four types of merits within the framework of the three functions, how can we not think here of the sin marked for Yima in the only postgāthic Avestan text which speaks of it, *Yašt* 19,33–34? This king's reign had been especially successful, we recall,[54] "until he lied, began to think the lying word, contrary to the truth." It may be that pride, *lectio facilior* of the royal temptations in sedentary and opulent societies, was substituted for the lie by a natural inclination, in India as well as in Iran after the *Avesta*: there is no Indo-Iranian term for pride, while the vocabulary of the truth and its opposite, with their complementary and derivative terms, their conceptual articulations and religious overtones, were already well established before the separation of the two groups of peoples. It may also be that these variations in the specification of the sins are more nominal than real. In Iranian ideology, and Indo-Iranian before it, the notion of "truth" is expressed by one or the other of the two words which in Vedic are *r̥tá* and *satyá*. Through an etymology that Vedic-speaking people surely still perceived, the second (derived from the present participle of the verb *as-*, "to be") expresses that the true is that which exists, that which is positive and not illusory; the first (past passive participle of the verb *ar-*, "to arrange, to harmonize") expresses that the true is that which conforms to order, whether cosmic or social or moral. From this second perspective, lying consists in not recognizing or in altering this order: such is the force behind the articulation, already present in Indo-Iranian tradition, between the opposite words: in Vedic *r̥tá* ~ *drúh*, and in Avestan *aša* (*arta*) ~ *druǰ*. This is so true that, in the language of Darius' inscriptions, *drauga*, the "lie," is essentially the attitude of rebels, of usurpers or potential usurpers who deceive the people by pretending to be "king" in place of Darius himself.[55] It is likely that, as early as *Yašt* 19, the lie, the lying word that Yima "began to think," was of this type: could one imagine a more serious alteration of the world order, and thus of the truth based on a conformity to it, than the neglect or the denial of God, the usurpation of divine honors? Thus, depending on one's point of view, psychological or metaphysical, Yima's sin probably is, and always was, both that of pride and that of untruth: pride within the secret of his own soul, a lie in the sight of men and God.[56]

Having observed these concordances, we must, of course, be attentive to the differences which exist between the Indian and

Iranian narratives. But it seems that several of these differences are adequately explained by the religious orientations of the two societies.

One of the most important dissimilarities concerns the point in the king's career at which the sin, with its consequences, occurs. In both cases it constitutes the final episode, but for the Indian king it takes place in heaven, in the course of his *post mortem* existence, and its consequences—losses and reparations—concern a destiny in the next world; for the Iranian king it is situated in this world, puts an end to a terrestrial life and a royal reign, and—according to the *Dēnkart*—three terrestrial figures benefit, with a view toward terrestrial actions, from the consequences. Similarly, in the Iranian legend, the reward of an ascent to heaven, preceding the sin, occurs during the reign and is no more than a voyage, conferring no permanent right to celestial residence and accorded by divine favor to the living Yima; whereas in India it is a routine ascent, made in expectation of a celestial position normally without end, by the man who has died in possession of a sufficient provision of merits. The result is that the initial effect of Yayāti's sin is the expulsion from heaven toward hell, while that of Yima, committed on earth, has no effect on a power of ascension that never has had a guaranteed future and which seems to have been exercised only once. This bundle of related differences can be sorted out if one takes account of the divergence of theologies—monotheism, polytheism—and also the individual eschatologies and, generally, ideas concerning the relations between the human and the divine. According to Mazdaism, no man, no matter how meritorious, can establish himself after death so intimately beside God; neither shall any man, after his death, be able to gain or lose merits, to change, voluntarily or involuntarily, the balance—whether good or bad—of his past actions, to modify the verdict which the divine officials have delivered on this balance: the elect and the damned are assured their felicity or woe for eternity. The Indian conceptions, as is natural in a polytheistic tradition, are more supple. And heaven, the many heavens, lodge beside and among the gods numerous eminent men who have escaped death or for whom death has been no more than the occasion for this happy emigration. But by way of compensation, their felicity can at any time be disrupted by but a single incident.

5. Yima, Yayāti, the Manipulation of Ages, and the Occupation of the World

At the beginning of this study we emphasized that the two episodes which make up Yayāti's story are connected rather loosely. The separate contents and the two sets of characters combine poorly.[57] This is true of the intrigues. But in the course of the preceding analyses the reader has easily discovered the principle of unity which justifies their association. In the first episode, through his sons, Yayāti provides lords, if not kings, to rule over the five parts of the inhabited world; in the second, he provides his grandsons with an opportunity to illustrate differentially the three functions whose harmony is necessary for the well-being of every group of men. In other words, he has almost realized the two fundamental tasks which one expects of a first king: the organization of the earth into its ethnic divisions, and the organization of society into its functional divisions.

"Almost," for in the form of the legend known to us, Yayāti actually founds neither of these divisions: they preexist. He distributes among his sons, the dutiful and the less dutiful, the peoples who were living before him in the central Fifth and in the four lands on the periphery; and, like us, he can only observe that, without his having to intervene or even to will it, his daughter's sons have become specialists in the three social functions. Is it possible that, in a more ancient form of the legend, the actions of this father of Pūru were truly those of a "first king," civilizer and founder of all, providing not only for the political distribution of the earth but for its peopling, and establishing its social order?

On the first point the *Mahābhārata* expresses itself ambiguously: when Yayāti, according to the words which have been attributed to him, contents himself with sending his four eldest sons into the outlying lands to rule there (some without the title of king), the poet concludes the episode with the distich already cited:

> from Yadu are born the Yādavas, from Turvasu the Yavanas are born, from Druhyu are born the Bhojas, and from Anu the *jātis* of Mlecchas.[58]

"The Yādavas," in the plural, could be a limitative designation of a lineage, the one to which Kṛṣṇa will belong; this is less likely for "the

Yavanas" and is excluded for the *mlecchajātayaḥ*, whether they be "families, varieties of Mlecchas (barbarians)," or "individual barbarians": thus besides sending out chiefs of his own race, Yayāti seems, as much as Noah, to be the ancestor of the various parts of humanity.

But as to the second point, no such ambiguity remains: Yayāti acquires, loses, and compensates for his merits in a fully constituted society of the arya type. Nothing justifies an assumption that this is an alteration of a more radical tradition, in which the four grandsons were not just the perfect models of the functions but their institutors, or the means of their institution. We can claim only that for those who were responsible for the text that we have in hand, it was, at all events, *no longer possible* to accept the theme in this form: how could a royal kṣatriya, whose daughter had married four royal kṣatriyas, have as his grandsons, beside a kṣatriya, two brahmans and a vaiśya? Like him, all are kings and kṣatriyas, only "oriented" according to the three functions in their meritorious activities. There remains the possibility that, without engendering the functional classes, he could have founded them by institution. But at his position in the dynastic line, well after Manu, there would no longer have been opportunity for him to do so.

Yima is more conservative on this second point. One of the constant features of his reign, although the parts of the *Avesta* which we still possess do not make it clear, is that he has established the division of the society into classes—priests, warriors, tiller-breeders, and artisans (such is in effect the catalogue of classes from the "later *Avesta*," the artisan class having become homogeneous with the three others).[59] But numerous traits lead one to think that his connection with the classes antedates this extension. Developing a point made by James Darmesteter, Émile Benveniste has shown that the singular plan of Yima's *vara*, the subterranean "reserve" in which God commands Yima to place the seeds first of mankind and then of all other living things, proves that it was destined for three human groups of unequal numerical importance which could only be those of the priests, the warriors, and the tiller-breeders.[60] Moreover, Benveniste and myself have given reasons for supposing that the tradition which made Zoroaster's three sons into the first priest, first warrior, and first tiller-breeder (the last, even more precisely, "chief of the agriculturalists in Yima's *vara*), is a retouch, for the greater glory of the prophet, of a pre-Zoroastrian tradition in which it was Yima, through his sons, who instituted the classes.[61]

As for the first point—distribution and perhaps peopling of the earth—if Yima's Avestan biography does not present its equivalent, it perhaps contains a substitute. But first we must observe a new correspondence between Yayāti and the Yima of this group of legends.

It will be recalled how Yayāti comes to send his four eldest sons far away from the "middle," and into the "border" lands.[62] Many explanations might be imagined as well as many sins, if these missions are punitive exiles. But the sin, in the variant of the first book of the *Mahābhārata*, is very precise: first condemned by the curse of Kāvya Uśanas to a sudden old age, Yayāti immediately obtains from the same Kāvya a privilege which, on the contrary, must assure him of a thousand years of youth. All he must do is find among his sons a volunteer who will exchange youth for old age. Only one of his sons, the last, accepts. He makes him his heir and, for a thousand years, leads a boy's existence, completely happy and dutiful besides, even when engaged in the most youthful frolics. As to his four oldest, he sends them out to the circumference to command peoples who are barbaric or corrupt. One important aspect of this episode is that Yayāti himself makes a connection here, and allows for an adjustment, with the story of Kāvya Uśanas.[63] As a result, it is thanks to him that this story is inserted as a long parenthesis in the ancestral history of the heroes of the poem. Kāvya Uśanas holds power over the ages: senescence and rejuvenation he controls at will. Such a power does not belong to Yayāti himself. First victimized and then protected by Uśanas, Yayāti becomes prematurely old, but then receives immediately, in the form of a deferment, a thousand years of youth. For these two stories to have been thus welded together, we must suppose that both, in certain of their more ancient variants, contained the theme of the manipulation of ages—active in one case, passive in the other—and, more precisely, the theme of the deferred old age. Elsewhere, as we have shown,[64] the Iranian Kay Ūs (Kavi Usa(δa)n) has conserved this trait, which after the silence of the *Avesta*, surfaces in the Pahlavi books of the ninth century and in the subsequent literature: this king is in charge of the mechanism which transforms old men into youths. Symmetrically, in Yima-J̌amšīd—to whom the second episode in Yayāti's tale has drawn our attention for other reasons—Iran presents the theme of deferred old age in its "passive" aspect.

That theme is, indeed, the most characteristic of the "good things" reported about him. When Yima was king, old age and death were suspended—in some texts, the only limit being the end of his lengthy reign, in others, for a term set in advance. Naturally it is not the result of personal action or power, as in the case of Kay Ūs: God, and he alone, achieves this miracle in his behalf, along with many others of like character (freedom from illness, superabundant food, etc.). A few examples taken from each period will suffice to show the consistency of the tradition.

Yasna 9,5 says:

> In the reign of the brave Yima, there was neither cold nor heat, there was neither old age nor death, nor demon-created envy. With the appearance of youths of fifteen years, father and son walked together as long as the man of good herds, Yima, son of Vivaṅhat, reigned.[65]

The Parsee *Rivāyat*, translated by Christensen, says that, after he had gone to seal up the gate of hell, J̌amšīd turned this day into a festival day, the Day of the Year, *nawrōz*:

> There was neither death nor old age, neither pain nor misfortune. . . . No one could distinguish father from son, for they were both equally young.[66]

In Tabarī, we read that on the day of the *nawrōz*, J̌im made it known to men that God had accorded him the following reward for his good conduct:

> that he could make them exempt from heat and cold, from sickness, old age, and envy. For three hundred years after the three hundred and sixteen years of his reign that had already passed, men remained in this state[. . .]. Indeed, God held all that apart from them. After this period, J̌im began to disdain God's grace toward him; he brought together spirits and men and told them that he was their king and that it was he who, by his power, had held sicknesses, old age, and death apart from them.[67]

Sometimes, but rarely, the benefit of these immunities is concentrated upon the king himself; thus in Belᶜamī:

> He possessed the empire for a thousand years, and, for this thousand years, he was not a moment inconvenienced or sick.[68]

The privilege that Yayāti owes to Uśanas is certainly not exactly the same. First of all, in its own terms, only Yayāti and his sons are concerned and entitled, individually, to be affected by it: the king's subjects are removed from it, and the order of the world is unaltered by the exception that it constitutes. Moreover, far from their appearing both as teen-agers, the father indistinguishable from the son, there is in this case an incompatibility between Yayāti's youth and that of his son Pūru: one of the two must grow old, Yayāti being able to annul his aging process only by transferring it onto Pūru, and Pūru being morally bound, as a dutiful son, to deprive himself of his youth for his father's sake. Still, having delayed his own senescence, Yayāti, like Yima, apparently enjoys a thousand years of youth without aging, for it certainly seems that, when the thousand years have passed, he returns the youth intact to its donor.

With all the variants of the tale, both in the case of Yima and in that of Yayāti, one of the results of this prolongued youth concerns the occupation and the human organization of the earth's surface. We have underlined the ambiguity expressed in the first book of the *Mahābhārata*,[69] which invites us to suppose the existence of a more ancient form of the narrative in which Yayāti, through his exiled sons, was in every way the ancestor of the "peoples of the circumference," if not of the center. Once inserted at the third rank in the canonical succession of kings, Yima no longer has to do this: one of his predecessors, the very first, had dispatched troops into the six *kišvars*, the fabulous regions which surround the central *kišvar* that is reserved for men.[70] But the suspension of old age and death involved him in another task concerning the center: in three stages he had to enlarge the earth—each time by a third of the original surface—to make a place upon it for the abnormal surplus population of men and animals. The event is recounted at length in *Vidēvdāt* 2,3–19, with formulary repetitions that assure the antiquity of the redaction, and also with obscurities in detail that fortunately do not affect the meaning of the passage.[71] Roughly speaking, it runs as follows: Ahura Mazdā charges Yima to become the protector, guardian, and overseer of his world; Yima accepts and, by virtue of this mission,[72] announces among other things that under his rule there will be neither cold wind nor hot wind, neither sickness nor death. Foreseeing an overpopulation crisis, Ahura Mazdā gives Yima two golden instruments, which, although interpreters disagree on their nature, serve him in any case to enlarge the earth.[73] At the end of sixty years,

> the earth was filled with small cattle and big cattle, with men [. . .] and more could find no place upon her, neither small cattle, big cattle, nor men.

Warned by Ahura Mazdā, Yima "advances toward the light, at the hour of noon, toward the path of the sun," and, with the two instruments, treats the earth in a certain way by commanding it to grow larger;

> and Yima enlarged the earth by a third more than it was at first. The little cattle, the big cattle, and men found there a home according to their liking.

The continued excess of health and vitality cannot help but pose the problem anew: at the end of six hundred years, and then at the end of nine hundred, Yima must perform the operation again, making no changes, always "toward the light, at noon, toward the path of the sun." And at last the habitable surface finds itself considerably increased. What would have happened if Yima had not lied one day and, in so doing, restored their regulative power to famine, sickness, old age, death, and the envy "created by the demons"?

Here it is not a matter of distributing the earth's portions among men: the men and the animals spread out apparently on their own into the new frontiers opened up to them. It no longer seems, given the identity of the formulas, that the added parts of the earth were produced entirely on the periphery: one has rather the impression of continuous extra leaves being extended from the Southern side. Might not this legend of Yima arresting old age and death and mechanically increasing the earth's surface be the learned elaboration of a more simple, pre-Zoroastrian tradition concerning the progressive peopling of habitable lands? And on its side, might not the legend of Yayāti disencumbered of his old age, installed for a thousand years in Pūru's youth and sending forthwith into certain "border lands" the other youths who did not wish to give him their youth, might it not be altered from a more simple tradition concerning the utilization of all lands, from the center outward, occasioned by an artificial surplus of the young? Different as they may be, they each join, for a sort of *uer sacrum*, two terms of the same kind, drawn from the same thematic stock: a manipulation of ages creating incompatibilities in the ancient homeland; and an extension of the occupied and organized part of the earth.[74]

Whatever may be the uncertain origin of this particular point, we see from the story of Yayāti and from this fraction of the story of Yima that well-structured traditions have been maintained: their biographies present several homologous episodes in the same order, one of which, in India and Iran, follows two parallel courses that are simply inverted toward the end. One thus glimpses, in the Indo-Iranian past, not just a type of hero, but an already constituted epic theme. To be sure, it would be pointless to compose a model prototype, as the differences are too great; but at least there does appear a firm enough model for a career as "first king."

6. Yima: Unitary or Synthetic Figure?

At this point, a problem faces us. We recalled in the Introduction that stories about Yima and stories about Yama seldom overlap. And yet we see that a considerable part of the career attributed in Iran to Yima corresponds to the career of another Indian king, one of a different name and one who has never been connected with Yama in any period. How are these findings to be interpreted? The Indo-Iranian prototype *Yama is attested to by the onomastic correspondence. Did he already have the complexity of his Iranian continuator, who then, in the form that we know him, contented himself with conserving the complexity in a Zoroastrian form while the Vedic and post-Vedic Yama reduced this great inheritance to a limited group of traits, leaving others available for a separate narrative which would be centered on a new name, Yayāti? Or, on the contrary, might Yima have added to the group of traits he had in common with the Vedic Yama, and which alone would have belonged to the Indo-Iranian *Yama, traditions that were originally independent and at first centered on another heroic name? The facts so far assembled evidently do not allow a decision. In support of the first thesis, one could maintain that, as Yayāti's name is not Indo-Iranian, it must be suspected of being secondary; and also that, as the Indian evolution observable from the *R̥gVeda* to Hinduism has inclined toward impoverishing Yama's endowment further, while at the same time confirming him in his divine position (his father Vivasvat disappears, becoming one of many names for the sun; no longer is he himself the "first to die," etc.), it is thus natural to suppose that a tendency in the same direction already existed between Indo-Iranian times and the *R̥gVeda*. In support of the second thesis, it could be pointed out that the Iranian traditions concerning Yima are not entirely coherent and even contain the trace of a contradiction, contrasting the very group of traits by which Yima corresponds to Yama to those by which he corresponds to Yayāti. Without being a king of the dead in a "beyond," as Yama is, Yima is nonetheless, at God's command and in expectation of an "end of the world," the constructor, and originally, it may be assumed, the lasting regent, or the subterranean *vara*, where, in what is indeed "another world," the specimens of humanity and more generally of all living beings are conserved. How can this conception be adjusted to that of the tragic end of Yima's reign in which he is conquered, falls, is tortured and slain on earth as a result of the sin (lie, pride) which made him lose for good his x^v*arənah*, his Glory, in three functional parts? May not this incoherence, awkwardly avoided by the texts, be an indication that Yima has annexed, in this second case, a distinct, preexistent tradition in which his destiny is hardly compatible with what it is in the first?

A new factor must now enter into the debate: Yama and Yayāti are not the only Indian figures to correspond to "portions of Yima." Another ancestor of the heroes of the *Mahābhārata*, Vasu Uparicara, also takes his place and justifies his name amid this rich comparative material.

3

VASU UPARICARA

1. Vasu Uparicara in the Genealogy of the Pāṇḍavas

Yayāti, the paternal ancestor of the Pauravas—that is, of the heroes of the *Mahābhārata*, so named after his son and successor Pūru—certainly does not have an uneventful reign, any more than did his father Nahuṣa or his great grandfather Purūravas, the lover of the "nymph" Urvaśī and rival of the Gandharvas. Nor are the great names that follow him in the dynasty any more given to tranquillity: one of his descendants will find the means to marry the daughter of the Sun, and this unusual couple will give birth to the last eponym of the line, Kuru. But on the whole, the line is largely human. At least, down to Pāṇḍu, the fathers or their legal substitutes engender their sons normally enough. It is the maternal ancestry of the Pāṇḍavas that is more fantastic.

It goes back to a king—himself born in the Paurava line—who, in Arthur Christensen's terminology, deserves no less that Yayāti the title of "first king," a title which he can support even though he does not rule the entire earth but only the fortunate kingdom of Cedi. He is the civilizer, the benefactor of his people, and has a reign that recalls the golden age. He lives with the gods, most notably Indra, in great familiarity. He has two names: one, Vasu, probably alludes to his great wealth; the other, Uparicara, literally "the one who circulates above," derives from one of his privileges. It is with him that we shall be concerned in this chapter. But let us first see how his blood came to flow in the veins of king Pāṇḍu and his brothers.[1]

Near his capital there flowed a beautiful river, too beautiful, in fact, since a neighboring peak, Mount Kolāhala, fell madly in love with her, barred her passage, and held her captive. King Vasu put an end to this violence: by a stamp of his foot, he made an opening in the mountain's side, and the river escaped. She had, however, become pregnant by her craggy ravisher. And when she had given birth to a pair of twins, she gratefully gave them to the king who had saved her. The king made the boy into the generalissimo of his army, and he married the girl, Girikā by name, some sort of "highland lass" who had inherited the beauty of her mother.

Vasu was a great hunter and a pious man. One day his wife Girikā, having bathed herself, let him know that she was now ready for fruitful embraces and was waiting for him. But just at that moment, the king's ancestors appeared before him, famished and asking for offerings; and they charged him to "go and kill game," *jahi mṛgān!* One can imagine the young king's perplexity: already brimful of desire for his wife, but first constrained to serve his ancestors. Not hesitating the least, he set out on the hunt. But an important part of his being remained under the spell of desire, the powerful demon so ably reinforced by the charm of the forests, the softness of the grass during his halts. Finally, it came to the point where he quickly had to tear off the leaf of a tree to collect his own semen. He did not want to waste this homage rendered to the Idea of his absent wife. So he summoned a falcon, which seized the leaf in its talons and accepted the mission of carrying it posthaste to the queen. The falcon took flight, but it was seen and attacked by another falcon, under the impression, no doubt, that it was carrying some more substantial prey. While they fought each other, the leaf dropped.

Now this duel took place over a river, the illustrious Yamunā, tributary to the divine Gaṅgā. In her waters there swam a fish, which, of course, was not really a fish but a celestial woman, an Apsaras, the beautiful Adrikā who had been reduced to this form by the curse of a brahman and condemned to live in the river until she brought a pair of human twins into the world. As soon as she perceived the falling leaf, she darted forth open-mouthed, swallowed it, and then continued to sport in the waters. Ten months later, some fishermen caught her and opened her up: from her stomach came forth twins, a boy and a girl. Somewhat surprised, the fishermen brought them to king Vasu—all this occurred in his kingdom—and did not conceal the circumstances of the birth. The king then took them in, while Adrikā, delivered from her curse, recovered her divine form and returned to heaven. The boy he made king Matsya, "Fish," who became an ancestor of a people of this name, who were to play a secondary role in the great confrontation of the *Mahābhārata*. As for the very beautiful daughter, she bore an unfortunate stigma: she discharged a strong odor of fresh sea fish. The king was thus constrained to part company with her, and he gave her back to a fisherman, saying to him "She will be yours, your daughter," *iyaṃ tava bhaviṣyati*. As virtuous as she was beautiful, she truly merited the name which was given her: Satyavatī, "the Truthful." But the maternal odor would not leave her. Fortunately, among fishermen this was no great handicap; so she was able to lead a normal life, rowing a fishing boat in the Yamunā to help her father, or the man whom she took to be her father.

One day a pilgrim, a very saintly man, passed along the river. It was the king Parāśara, making the rounds of the numerous hermitages on its banks. From a distance he saw the beautiful oarswoman and felt an imperious urge to know her better. He approached and told her bluntly of his desire. The girl made a pleasing response: "You wouldn't," she said, "with all these hermits looking at us . . ." But soon, by the force of his penitence, he raised up a thick fog which, by enclosing them, was as good as a private room. Seeing that matters had taken a serious turn, Satyavatī raised a compelling objection: she was not free, she had a father; if she yielded, how would she dare show herself again before him? In such cases, the ascetics in Indian fables have an ever-ready response; they make a promise and, moreover, scrupulously keep it: after the embrace, or after the childbirth which follows from it, the young girl will become a virgin again, without the least trace of her compliance. The intelligent Satyavatī thus resolved to give in, but she had the presence of mind to seek indemnity in the most suitable way: she solicited a favor of her own choosing. The ascetic promised again to grant her wish, and she chose that her fishy odor be transformed into a marvelous perfume. This was a mere trifle for the ascetic, and when, having been satisfied, he left his momentary partner and went on piously to the next hermitage, he left her pregnant and perfumed. Indeed, terribly perfumed: she charmed the nostrils for such distances as are reserved, in the west, for the calculations of astronomers. And terribly pregnant too: she carried in her womb one of the greatest sages, one of the most potent ṛṣis, Vyāsa, who as soon as he was born, took leave of his mother to go into the forest and devote himself to a life of faultless penitence. On his departure, he told her that if she ever needed him, under any circumstances, she had only to call his name and he would appear before her. Among other services for mankind, Vyāsa was to be credited with putting in order not only the four Vedas, but the *Mahābhārata*, which is the fifth. Later he would communicate this knowledge to several disciples, notably Vaiśampāyana, who, in his turn, was to recite the immense poem at the time of the so called "snake sacrifice," celebrated by one of the first descendants of the Pāṇḍavas, Janamejaya, the great grandson of Arjuna.[2]

Before composing this poem, however, Vyāsa had to produce—in the most literal, material meaning of the word—its subject matter and give birth to its heroes. At the most dramatic moment, Satyavatī and her ascetic son join forces and together take care of this problem. This is how they did it.[3]

Having now become deliciously fragrant, Satyavatī was seen, smelled, and desired by king Śāntanu, a descendant of Yayāti, thus a full-blooded Paurava and Kaurava, whom the supreme God had chosen to be the grandfather of Pāṇḍu and the great-grandfather of the five Pāṇḍavas. From a previous wife, the river goddess Gaṅgā, Śāntanu had already had one son of great merit, and at first he resisted his passion for the beautiful girl in the boat. But seeing him despair, this son took the initiative in arranging his remarriage. He sought out the fisherman, the beautiful girl's foster father, then called the "king of fishermen." His mission was a success; but at what a price! The fisherman, letting it be understood that Satyavatī was of high birth, would consent to the marriage only on the condition that her future son would be recognized as the sole heir to the throne. And, the better to assure this agreement, he demanded further that his interlocutor, the son by the first wife, should renounce not only the assertion of his rights to the throne, but also any idea of marriage or of becoming a father. The prince, his father's matchmaker, solemnly undertook these two obligations and, under these circumstances, received from the gods the name Bhīṣma, "the Terrible"; for his double sacrifice had been terrible indeed. He also received, from his father, a privilege which entitled him to the extraordinary role which he has in the *Mahābhārata*: that of not dying, despite all wounds, until the day he himself decides to die.

Satyavatī thus marries Śāntanu and bears him two sons, successive heirs to the throne and younger half-brothers—without knowing him—of the sage Vyāsa.[4] Shortly after their father's death, the first falls in battle without having had children. Similarly childless, the second dies of consumption. The dynasty seems condemned to immediate extinction and, with it, the cult of the ancestors, since, bound by his renunciations, Bhīṣma can become neither a king nor a father. But Indian casuistry has provided for such an eventuality: it is enough for children to be engendered in the name of the dead; they may then be credited to them and thus inherit all their rights and duties. But who should father these children? The nearest relative. Here again, due to his second renunciation, Bhīṣma, half-brother to the dead king by their father, is unfit and excluded. Fortunately, however, there is the ascetic Vyāsa, half-brother to the dead princes by their mother, who has not been paralyzed by any renunciation and who has promised his mother to appear before her immediately, upon a simple call, to extricate her from any trouble. With Bhīṣma's agreement, Satyavatī calls Vyāsa, and, by each of the two wives of the deceased king, Vyāsa engenders a son. But, as the result of a most significant fate, each baby is marked with a defect: because the first queen closed her eyes when she saw the hairy man who had been destined as her partner, her son Dhṛtarāṣṭra is born blind; because the second queen turned pale under the same test, her son Pāṇḍu is born with a white face. A third effort is the least successful: the first queen, when it is her turn again, cannot resolve herself to respond to Vyāsa's embrace and has a slave act as a stand-in; consequently, the highly virtuous son born of this union, Vidura, is a sort of bastard, of mixed blood. Among these three sons, only one, whose stigma is minor, is fit to rule: this is the second, the pallid-faced Pāṇḍu. Raised with his brothers by their uncle Bhīṣma, he indeed becomes king. For his own sons—putative sons, but that is another story—Pāṇḍu has, in succession, the five "Pāṇḍavas," the good heroes of the poem, while the blind Dhṛtarāṣṭra, Pāṇḍu's elder brother, at one stroke fathers a hundred sons, the poem's evil heroes.

So it is that, through Satyavatī, Vasu Uparicara turns out to be the ancestor, and a recent one at that, of the Pāṇḍavas and the

Dhārtarāṣṭras: excited by the thought of the twin daughter of a river and a mountain, he discharges his semen, which is swallowed by a nymph-turned-fish; and the fully human daughter, a twin again, who is drawn from the latter's stomach, gives birth, in two successive states of virginity, to the real grandfather, and then to the putative grandfather, of the two groups of cousins.

For some lower organisms, natural history describes cycles of reproduction that are even more complicated. But for human beings, at least among the Indo-Europeans, I know of none more remarkable, not even the succession of twins, some born of plants, which the erudite Zoroastrianism of the Pahlavi books places between the primordial man and the first king. I recall it here briefly, according to the *Bundahišn*, not because the two traditions are genetically related (they are obviously not), but because their comparison confirms the impression that Vasu Uparicara stands at the head of a genealogy that is as fantastic as anthropogonies can be in other contexts.[5] A third of the semen of the primordial man, Gayomart, killed by Ahriman, is put on deposit under the earth; at the end of forty years a plant, *rīvās*, emerges from it, a plant two stems of which produce the twins Mašya and Mašyānī, "Mortal" male and "Mortal" female, a boy and a girl who themselves give birth to another pair, from which a third is born, who, likewise by pairs, begets the various kinds of beings who populate the seven parts of the world, notably—through Hōšang and his sister Gūzak—the Iranians.

2. Vasu Uparicara, the Crystal Chariot and the Festival of Indra's Garland

Aside from this picturesque but fortuitously begotten family line, Vasu Uparicara is the hero of several coherent legends which show him ending a particularly happy life with a sin followed by a punishment. A section of the first book of the *Mahābhārata* gives a lengthy description of the course of his reign,[6] while his end is recounted by several passages from the "encyclopedic books," the twelfth and thirteenth.

The poem does not name the parents of this virtuous prince. It says only that, *indropadeśāt*, "under instruction from Indra," he conquered, *jagrāha*, the delightful kingdom of Cedi, but that then, renouncing the use of arms, he retired into the forest to devote himself to austerities. In the face of this type of conduct, the gods are always on the alert: they quickly suspect a great ascetic of ambitions which threaten their supremacy. So, despite the purity of Vasu's intentions, they feared that he wanted to dethrone Indra and become their king. For once, they sent him no Apsarases as temptresses. Indra chose to conduct the affair man to man, so to speak. Accompanied by the gods, he presented himself and told him that a king who prefers asceticism to his duties does not conform to *dharma*, the very foundation of the world; that the *dharma* of the king is to protect the *dharma* of the world, and, consequently, that his eternal salvation was at stake. Despite their difference in rank, it was as *sakhā*, as friends or colleagues, that the "celestial" was speaking to the "terrestrial," urging him to return to this kingdom of Cedi so rich, as Indra tirelessly described it, in animals and grains, minerals and precious stones, climate and fertility; whose inhabitants, he said, are perfectly virtuous, never telling a lie even in jest, and observing the distinctions of class; where sons honor their fathers and peasants take care of their oxen. Then, to these praises of the land of Cedi, Indra added further enticements. He gave a series of presents to the hermit-king:

> "Let there be nothing in the three worlds," he said to him, "that remains unknown to you. Given by me, a great chariot of divine crystal, privilege of the gods, capable of circulating in space, awaits you. Alone among all mortals, riding on this marvelous chariot, you will circulate in mid-air like a god endowed with a body.
>
> "I give you a garland made of unfading lotuses: it assures victory. In combat, it will make you invulnerable to missiles. It will be your insignia: blessed, incomparable, grand, it will be known here as 'Indra's Garland.'"
>
> In addition, the god, slayer of Vṛtra, also gave him a bamboo pole, a precious gift destined for the protection of virtuous men.

This pole is to have an important future: at the end of a year, commemorating these precious gifts with an anniversary festival, the king of Cedi planted it in the earth to honor Indra; and since then, all kings imitate him.[7] Golden cloths, garlands, and all sorts of ornaments are suspended from this pole, and it is covered with perfumes. The god deigned to come in person to receive the offerings of the first celebrant. He declared that, in the future, for all those who would repeat the rite, prosperity and victory, *srīr vijayaśca*, would be assured, that this good fortune would extend to their subjects—and subsequent experience shows that the god, statistically speaking, kept his word. As to the crystal chariot, bringing admiration from the Gandharvas and the Apsarases, the king used it as a spaceship; and it is this device that earned him his second name, *Upari-cara* "ὑπέρ-πογος."

He had five sons, excellent subjects in every respect. Being himself *samrāj*, "universal monarch"—and so he will appear from now on—he installed them in as many various kingdoms, *nānārājyeṣu*. For only one son, Bṛhadratha, is the realm named: that of Magadha;[8] but all are said to have given their names to lands and cities. It is remarkable that one of them is called Yadu, a name which, as we have seen,[9] is already used, and chiefly used in the epic, for one of the five sons of Yayāti.

3. Vasu Uparicara, the Lie, and the Butchered Food

There seems to be nothing to threaten the career of this royal friend of the gods. Yet, as we learn from other books of the poem, this very quality, or position, brings on his misfortune; not by an impulse of revolt against the gods, but, on the contrary, by an excess of complacency toward the gods. As usual, one finds several variants, but they agree on the nature of the fault and the punishment: in an important matter, Vasu Uparicara did not tell the truth, and, as a result, he fell from heaven to earth, indeed, right into the earth. But he told the lie in unusual circumstances, the question being whether or not it was permissible to eat meat or, more generally, to sacrifice animals and thus feed the gods with meat.

In the thirteenth book, the second of the encyclopedic books, in which are accumulated the interminable teachings that Bhīṣma gives on a bed of arrows before he allows himself to die, a whole section is devoted to the merits attached to abstaining from meat and the sin committed by those who eat it.[10] Eminent authorities are cited: Manu, Mārkaṇḍeya. To be sure, exceptions are foreseen in at least one text, and that a composite one. According to some, the prohibition would pertain only to meat coming from animals slain unnecessarily, or not previously purified. But it is best, says the same text, to accept the rule in all its strictness and to abstain from the flesh of every creature. And then comes the etiology. Formerly, beset with doubt about the legitimacy of butchered food, the ṛṣis raised the question in consultation with Vasu, king of Cedi:

and Vasu, although he knew that meat could not be eaten, answered that it could be.

At that very instant, he fell from heaven to earth. Then, having repeated this wrong answer, he sank beneath the ground.

In the twelfth book the story is told with many more details, and the problem under debate concerns not only slaughtered food but animal sacrifices in general.[11] Moreover, at the end, Vasu is saved, restored—like Yayāti through his grandsons—here by the intervention of Viṣṇu.

Once upon a time, the gods and the ṛṣis had a dispute about a point of divine law. The gods, directly interested in the matter, maintained that the object of sacrifice, *aja*, should remain, as it was traditionally, the goat, the word *aja*, in fact, being the ordinary name for the goat itself. The ṛṣis, contesting this position and probably pushed into an *aggiornamento* by the progress of the times, quibbled over the word *aja*: analyzing it as a compound, *a-ja*, "not-born," they maintained that it refers to the seeds of plants and that, as a result, the gods should content themselves with offerings of barley. The discussion quickly grew heated, as it often does among ritualists. Suddenly the two parties, the conservatives and the progressives, saw Vasu Uparicara coursing through the atmosphere at the controls of his crystal chariot. With common accord, they took him as their arbiter, and the ṛṣis confronted him with the two doctrines. Knowing the wishes of the gods, the king decided in their favor: sacrifices, he determined, should be celebrated with animal victims. Then the ṛṣis punished him:

"Since you have taken the side of the gods," they said, "you will fall from the sky. From this day you will lose the power which you have to circulate in the air! By our curse, you will sink far below the surface of the earth!"

Indeed, the unfortunate king dropped to the earth immediately, and found himself at the bottom of a deep pit. But the gods did not abandon the one who had sinned to serve them. To be sure, they could not annul the curse of such saintly men, but they fed him in his open-topped tomb, taking care that he should suffer no further ills and that he should not lose his strength. For his own part, taking inspiration from the example given by Trita in a well-known sacred narrative (*itihāsa*), Vasu, at the bottom of his well, silently celebrated an act of worship which earned him the sympathy of the "over-god," Nārāyaṇa-Viṣṇu. The latter sent the bird Garuḍa, and on its back Vasu reascended triumphantly through the atmosphere up into the world of Brahmā.

Almost the same account, this time without the final redemption, is summarized briefly in the fourteenth book.[12] In the course of a sacrifice offered to Indra, the ṛṣis, filled with compassion at the sight of the victims about to be killed, proposed to the gods that henceforth they should only present them with grain offerings. Indra, a carnivore, indignantly refused. And there followed a long discussion which the two parties agreed to terminate by the arbitration of Vasu.

> "Blessed man," the ṛṣis said to him, "What is the Vedic teaching concerning sacrifices? Is it preferable to celebrate them with animals, or with grains and juices?"

Vasu's answer was a hasty one. He did not weigh the pros and cons or examine the arguments of the two briefs, but heedlessly declared:

> "Of the two materials, sacrifices may be celebrated with the one that lies close at hand, no matter which it may be."[13]

This response, which was a lie, caused him to be hurled into the subterranean regions of Rasātala.

4. Yima, the Crystal Chariot, and the Festival of the New Year

This concentration of episodes concerning Vasu Uparicara constitutes a story that runs parallel to a sequence which, in Iran, is once again connected with Yima-Jamšīd and which is not recovered either in the myth of Yama or in the story of Yayāti. Or rather, Yayāti and Vasu are comparable only at the beginning of their careers and as a general type. Each is a prosperous king ruling over a prosperous kingdom. Each has five sons to whom each distributes "diverse" realms. Each—although with some different implications—is called a *samrāj*. Thus each displays the traits of the "first king." This is all, and its only importance for us is that it guarantees that the two figures are indeed on the same level, and are also on the same level as Yima, the Iranian figure with whom we compare them.

Vasu Uparicara receives from Indra—to use as he wishes during his own lifetime—a chariot in which he can circulate through space. To be sure, celestial chariots are a commonplace accessory in the fantasy land of Indian myths, and it is quite frequent for the gods, notably Indra, to send their cars, with or without driver, to a privileged mortal whom they wish to call to heaven for a visit or, sometimes, for good. At the end of one of the variants of the story of Yayāti's redemption, the five chariots which appear before the four grandsons and their grandfather are of the type.[14] Uparicara's vehicle is different: it is a gift made by a god to a man, to a king who still continues to reign over the earth. It is a gift which he enjoys "alone among mortals" and a gift which has enough importance during his lifetime for the surname derived from it to have been grafted onto his name.

Moreover, this gift is but part of a threefold presentation. Another part, the bamboo pole is immediately put to use by the king to establish the great annual festival in honor of Indra, probably a new year celebration,[15] intended to promote the prosperity of the king and his realm and to assure him superiority over his enemies. This same benefit is also guaranteed directly to Vasu Uparicara by the garland of victory and invulnerability called Indramālā, "garland of Indra."

Now these two traits—the possession of the celestial chariot and the founding of the New Year festival—are also, and in connection with each other, characteristic of Yima, if not in the official Zoroastrian texts, at least in the lateral tradition which has produced the works of the Muslim period. Thus in Tabarī: after J̌amšīd had delivered all sorts of lessons of civilization to men,

> by his command a glass car was constructed for him, and the devils entered it; and he mounted it and proceeded in this car to go through the atmosphere in a single day from Demavend, the land where he resided, to Babylon. That was the day of Ōhrmazd in the month of Fravardīn, and because of this miracle, of which men were witnesses, namely the voyage through the air which he undertook in this manner, they made that day into the New Year's Day (*nawrōz*), and he enjoined them to celebrate that day and the five succeeding days as a festival and to enjoy themselves during that time.

And on the sixth day, which was the day of Xurdāt, he wrote to men that the conduct he had followed among them was pleasing to God and that the reward which was accorded to him by God was this: that he would render them free from heat and cold, from disease, from old age, and from envy.[16]

So again in al Thaᶜalibi, after the enumeration of the meritorious civilizing deeds of J̌amšīd:

J̌im had an ivory and teakwood chariot constructed and had it covered with brocade; having mounted it, he ordered the demons to carry him on their shoulders in the region between heaven and earth. Thus he traveled in the air, from Demavend to Babylon in a single day. This was the day of Ōhrmazd in the month of Fravardīn, the first day of spring, which is the beginning of the year, the time of renovation, when the earth revives after its torpor. Men said: "This is a new day, a happy festival, a real power, an extraordinary king!" And they made this day, which they called *nawrōz*, their principal festival; they praised God for having made their king attain such a degree of greatness and power, and they rendered him thanks for all he had accorded them through the good fortune of this king and under the umbrage of his rule, in matters of ease, well-being, security, and wealth. They celebrated this auspicious festival by eating and drinking, by making their musical instruments resound, and by giving themselves up entirely to diversions and pleasures.[17]

And in the Chronology of Birunī:

When J̌amšīd had taken possession of the royal power, he renovated the religion, and this undertaking, which was accomplished at the *nawrōz*, was called "the new day"; and this day was established as a feast day, although it had already been celebrated before this epoch. And, as to the reason why this day became a feast day, it is also told that J̌amšīd, after having had a car constructed, mounted it on that day, and that the spirits and demons carried him in the atmosphere from Demavend to Babylon in one day. People also made this day a feast day on account of the miracle which they had seen, and they introduced the custom of playing with the seesaw to imitate J̌amšīd.[18]

And finally in Ferdowsi:

Then he had a throne constructed, inlaid with precious stones, and at his bidding the *dīv* lifted it up and carried it from the earth to the vault of the sky. The powerful king sat there like the sun shining in the firmament. Men gathered around his throne, astonished at his great fortune, and poured out their jewels upon him, and they called this the new day (*nawrōz*): that was the first day of the new year, the first (*Hurmaz*) of the month of Fravardīn. On this day the body used to take rest from work, the heart forgot its hatreds. The great, in their joy, prepared a feast; they called for wine, for cups, and for singers, and this glorious festival has been conserved from that time to ours in memory of the king.[19]

5. Yima, the Lie and Butchered Food

This superhuman power, and every kind of power, as we have seen, was lost by Yima-J̌amšīd through a sin which, according to the whole of the Muslim tradition, was pride. In his pride, the king denied God, and took credit himself for the miracles which, through him, God alone had initiated. But, as will be recalled, in the only text conserved from the postgāthic Avesta that speaks of it, the sin was defined differently, although none too precisely: one day the text says, "he lied, and began to think the lying thought contrary to truth."[20] Accordingly, he lost his *x*ᵛ*arənah* and his royalty and "lived hidden" on earth while awaiting the saw of the assassin. It is, of course, a lie, the same sin, which causes Uparicara, to fall from the sky onto, then under, the earth.

As to the Gāthās, Yima is mentioned there only once, allusively. He is spoken of as a sinner, a criminal (*Yasna* 32,8).[21] The text has been interpreted, construed in many ways as is customary for nearly every line of the Gāthās; but today there seems to be a general, if not unanimous, agreement on the most probable meaning of the passage. Here is the translation by Jacques Duchesne-Guillemin:

> Among these sinners, we know, is Yama, son of Vīvaṅhat,
> Who to please our people made them eat the flesh of the ox [*gāuš bagā*].
> In thy decision, O Wise One, I shall be apart from these.[22]

This description of Yima's fault belongs to a tradition in which eating meat is not always considered as a fault at all. Christensen has drawn from the Pahlavi and Sanskrit commentaries on *Yasna* 9,4, which teach that Haoma—the god Haoma, the sacrificial plant personified—was immortal because of its own religious activity and not in the manner of those "who have eaten meat which was given to them by Yima": from which it results, he concludes, that in certain Zoroastrian circles it was still admitted that under this king the privilege of not dying, which men enjoyed, resulted from animal food.[23] In any case, the most ancient text, *Yasna* 32, is very probably speaking of the introduction of this practice, the teaching of it, as a crime of Yima, although one cannot tell from the merely allusive verse of the gāthā whether, in the pre-Zoroastrian tradition to which it refers, the "crime" in question was connected with, was the cause of, Yima's disgrace, or whether, as on so many points, the reformer limited himself to predicating as a crime a practice unreservedly accepted until his time which he condemned and wished to abolish.[24]

In summary, Yima-J̌amšīd, king of a golden age, received by divine favor various objects,[25] then had the privilege of coursing through the sky in a chariot (less perfected than Uparicara's, for it is still demonically propelled); and on that occasion he instituted the annual royal festival of the *nawrōz̧*. He taught men to eat meat, whether it was considered a good or an evil. Then he sinned, and one of the specifications for his sin, the most ancient, is that he lied with premeditation. As a result of this sin he was hurled from his throne, dead with a stay of execution, a sentence which, barring exceptional texts,[26] is without pardon. These traits and episodes are articulated differently than in the story of Uparicara, and they are saturated with a different theology. But the same set of traits and episodes are found in both stories—are, indeed, the basic material of both stories—and for the most part they are too singular to have become fortuitously attached, in similar combinations, to two separate figures.

We are now a little better equipped to examine the problems posed at the end of the preceding chapter. Without imposing an incontestable solution, the plurality of the Indian counterparts to Yima—Yama, Yayāti, Uparicara—this parceling out of his rich career into more reduced and more coherent units, strongly suggests—rather than establishes—the hypothesis that it was in Iran that a variety of materials, formerly separated, became concentrated upon a single figure. I have already called attention to the *vara*,[27] Yima's subterranean enclosure which, in this perspective, would be the major element to survive from the meager tradition concerning the original Indo-Iranian *Yama. It appears to have been linked, through an awkward alteration, to a terrestrial reign of Yima's which, judging from the Indian Yama, was of no concern to the Indo-Iranian, prehistoric *Yama, and which, in Iran itself, came to a terrestrial end, ignominious and irreparable, incompatible with Yima's position as ruler in the enclosure under the earth. We can also emphasize that the Iranian texts seem hesitant on the very points where, according to our hypothesis, materials from diverse origins have been drawn together. For example, the institution of the New Year's festival—generally connected with the voyage of the celestial chariot as is the founding of Indra's festival in the story of Uparicara—occasionally appears linked to, and explained by, another event: the proclamation by J̌amšīd of the favor, granted him by God, that death, old age, etc., will cease during his reign. And in turn, the equivalent of this privilege is found neither in the story of Uparicara nor in the myths of Yama, but rather, more limited in its application, in the legend of Yayāti. Such hesitations in the stowage of some episodes is perhaps a mark of their primitive independence. All this, however, is only a record of personal impressions: the question, like so many in our field, remains open.

4

MĀDHAVĪ

1. Gālava, Yayāti, and the Four Sons of Mādhavī

The story of Yayāti, as presented in the first book of the *Mahābhārata*, contains only two episodes, those which we have been considering: the stories of his youth and difficulties, with his wife, his awesome father-in-law, and his own sons; and then, after his death and his installation in heaven, the story of his fall and his restoration, the latter made possible by the generosity of his daughter's sons. Repeating the final episode with several variations, the fifth book provides it with a very useful introduction, for in the first book these four grandsons appear abruptly, with nothing to account for them. Their birth, recounted at length in the fifth book, takes its place in Yayāti's life as an intermediary episode, a necessary one even though Yayāti makes only a few appearances in it. This narrative, of the highest interest, is moreover pleasantly set forth.[1]

As often happens in India, the introduction has been furnished with an introduction of its own, which at first disorients the reader but is soon seen to be necessary. We are this time in a hermitage where the former king, the kṣatriya Viśvāmitra, the most illustrious of the exceedingly rare persons who have been able to change their social class, is in the throes of attempting to promote himself into a brahman, having been convinced by a previous adventure, in which he found himself opposed to the sage brahman Vasiṣṭha, of the superiority of priests over warriors, of austerity over arms.[2] One day, while Viśvāmitra was devoting himself to the most severe penances, the god Dharma, having assumed the appearance of Vasiṣṭha, presented himself to him and, in order to test him, told him that he was hungry. Having nothing ready, Viśvāmitra started to cook a mixture of rice, milk, and sugar. But this required a certain amount of time, during which he was not able to attend to his guest. Feigning impatience, the latter ate the food which other neighboring ascetics brought to him, and, when Viśvāmitra approached, the dish balanced on his head, his only thanks were the words: "I have already eaten, wait here!" And the guest went away. Viśvāmitra waited heroically: on the same spot, stiff as a post, supporting the dish of rice pudding on his head with upraised arms. A younger ascetic, Gālava by name, recognizing this as an occasion for him to attain great merits, began to serve and care for this living column. After a hundred years, Dharma-Vasiṣṭha reappeared and accepted the dish, still, after this long wait, warm and tasty. Dharma ate it. And then, satisfied, he fulfilled Viśvāmitra's dream: from a kṣatriya, he transformed him into a brahman. Returned to normal life, the new priest expressed his gratitude to his disciple Gālava and gave him his leave. But Gālava knew the corpus of religious law; at the end of a novitiate, every disciple must offer a present, a payment, to his spiritual master. He thus asked Viśvāmitra what he desired. Under the circumstances, Viśvāmitra considered himself adequately paid by a hundred years of service: he refused to answer. And it is here that Gālava committed a fatal error: he grew obstinate, he repeated the question several times. Losing patience, Viśvāmitra named his price: "Give me eight hundred steeds, each of moonlike whiteness with one black ear apiece. Go, hurry up!"[3]

Cālava withdrew, in desperation: where could he find, how could he purchase, eight hundred such peculiar horses? In a long meditation, he pursued his thoughts from the most reliable moral principles to the point of considering death: one should not be ungrateful, he told himself; one should not fail to keep a promise; one who has lied can expect neither posterity nor power, etc. Fortunately, at the end of all this, he decided only to entrust himself to the protection of Viṣṇu. And just at that moment there appeared before him the celestial bird Garuḍa, messenger and mount of Viṣṇu himself. Although it is not explained how, Garuḍa happened also to be the friend of the brahman in difficulty, and, as is the duty of a prosperous friend, he looked after him. "I have already spoken to Viṣṇu about you," he said, "and he has given me time off. Come quickly. I will carry you to the other side of the ocean, to the ends of the earth."

In an enormously long monologue of a hundred ślokas, Garuḍa, so that Gālava can choose advisedly the direction of their journey, first made his unfortunate friend listen to a detailed description of everything one encounters at each of the cardinal points. Finally, Gālava declared himself in favor of the east, which, in highly laudatory terms, had been the first presented to him. Then they began a long ride, in which the comic mingles with the mystical, told in the manner that Lucian might have told it, had he been respectful of the sacred. Gālava is made dizzy by the speed and the altitude, and his cries are like those heard at the fairground from people on the ferris wheel, while Garuḍa, being a bird, makes fun of him. But there are adventures in store for the bird too. Toward evening they set down on the peak of a mountain, and there they receive the pleasant hospitality of a brahman woman who seats them, feeds them, and gives them a place to sleep. Upon waking up, however, the divine bird has lost his feathers. Gālava, who takes badly to the idea of ending his days atop these steep cliffs, interrogates him sternly: such a disgrace must surely be the punishment for some gross sin! Indeed, Garuḍa does have a confession to make: during the night, he entertained the thought of an abduction—without the least trace of lasciviousness, to be sure: seeing so perfect a brāhmaṇī, he had been pierced with the desire to lift her up and carry her off to the world of his master Viṣṇu. Now he asks her pardon, and, as good as she is virtuous, the brāhmaṇī absolves him; he recovers his plumage and again sets off with his passenger through the aerial corridors of heaven.

But it turns out that Garuḍa is not as sure of himself as he has let it appear; their journey across the world is one of pure agitation. As luck would have it, they cross paths with none other than Viśvāmitra, who reminds Gālava of his promise and demands an early payment. Garuḍa must then admit his helplessness: in order to acquire such horses, one must have fabulous wealth—those untold riches in the bowels of the earth over which Kubera, flanked by formidable aides, keeps a jealous watch. He sees only one solution: they must go and find an especially rich and prosperous king and ask him for alms. And he names a king, a personal friend, showering him with praises which, once we have learned who he is, seem perfectly fitting: it is Yayāti, our Yayāti:

"There is a king born in the lunar line," says the bird. "We shall seek him out, for he is the richest man on earth. This royal sage named Yayāti, is the son of Nahuṣa. He is of true valor. Urged by me, solicited by you, he will give alms, for he has immense resources, as much as the divine lord of wealth. With what he will give you, O sage, pay what you owe to your *guru*."[4]

Garuḍa carries his brahman friend to his royal friend's capital, sets forth to Yayāti their present difficulty, and requests his help. The king, he adds, will not take a total loss: after Gālava pays off his *guru*, he will retreat into the forest, there to amass a wealth of spiritual treasures, some portion of which he will not fail to transfer to his benefactor. Yayāti reflects. He is sensitive to his winged friend's plea, appreciative of Gālava's merits, and, moreover, how can he, the pious and generous king, refuse to give alms? But the alms he does give are unexpected. He owns none of the exceedingly rare horses, but he does have a daughter, wondrously beautiful, perfectly virtuous, whose hand is ever sought by men, gods, and even demons. Let alone eight hundred white steeds with one black ear apiece, he says, princes of the earth are ready to give entire kingdoms in order to obtain her hand. "Take her," he says to Gālava, "take my daughter Mādhavī. My only desire is to have a grandson by her."[5] Gālava and Garuḍa then make off with the girl who has just been ceded to them, and the bird cries out joyously: "We now hold the door to the horses!"[6] How could he foresee how narrow this door would be? He thus departs, with Gālava's permission, and leaves the sage entirely on his own to work out the means whereby this feminine capital, which he has procured for him, can be transformed into horses.

Gālava and Mādhavī first make their way to the king of Ayodhya, Haryaśva of the race of Ikṣvāku, the model prince with an army consisting of four kinds of forces under his command, a well-filled treasury and an abundance of grain at his disposal, devoted to brahmans, and loved by his subjects. But this happy man suffers from a serious lack: he has no descendants. Gālava introduces his charming ward and makes his proposal: "This maiden of mine, O Indra of kings, is made to increase lineages by her childbirths. Accept her as your wife, Haryaśva, by paying her price. I will tell you how much it will be, and you will decide."[7]

Haryaśva reflects for some time. He ardently desires to get a son, and the partner proposed to him is truly to his liking. Then he decides:

"The six parts of the body," he says, "which shall be high, this girl has high; the seven which shall be delicate, are delicate; the three which shall be deep, are deep in her; and the five which shall be red, are red. . . .[8] Upon her she has many favorable signs and will surely have many children; she can even give birth to a son destined to become a universal king.[9] Consider my resources, O noble brahman, and tell me the price of this marriage."

Gālava does not hesitate:

"Give me eight hundred horses of good stock, of lunar color, each with a black ear, and this beautiful, long-eyed girl will be the mother of your children, as the fire-stick, when rubbed, kindles a fire!"

Upon hearing these words, the king becomes sorrowful; but he is already overcome with desire. "I have thousands of other horses," he says, "all worthy of being offered in sacrifice. But I have only two hundred of the kind you want. Grant that for this price I may father a single son in this girl."[10] Far short of his mark, this leaves Gālava in a quandary. Passive and silent up to now, the girl Mādhavī suddenly takes charge of the negotiations over her own purchase:

"A brahman," she said, "granted me the privilege of recovering my virginity after every childbirth. Therefore, give me away to this king and accept his good horses. In this way, I will make up the sum of your eight hundred horses with four kings, for whom I will give birth to four sons. Thereby, O best of brahmans, collect the total needed to pay your *guru*.[11] Such is my idea, but it is up to you to decide."

How can he hesitate? Without even answering the ingenious girl, he says to the king:[12]

"Accept the girl for a fourth of her price, Haryaśva, O best of men, and beget only one son!"

The king no longer wavers. When the time has elapsed, he has only to give his son a name: Vasumanas, the prince "with the spirit turned toward wealth." The poet notes in passing that, later on, he would fully merit this appellation for he would be rich among the rich and a generous giver of riches.[13] Gālava does not waste a moment: as soon as the child is born, he comes to reclaim the mother:

"Here, O king, is a son born to you, a boy equal to the sun. It is time, O best of men, for us to go to another king for alms."[14]

Haryaśva does not protest or hesitate: he knows very well that it will not be easy to obtain the required horses. Heroically, he returns Mādhavī who, a virgin once again,[15] abandons the splendor of this royal court to follow Gālava. The latter entreats the king to keep the two hundred horses on deposit, and then leaves.

The scene is repeated with a second king, Divodāsa, surnamed Bhīmasena, "of the terrible army," who, like his predecessor, has no sons. This time all goes smoothly: the king has already heard about these curious marriages and is eager to be included on the list. But, like Haryaśva, he can only pledge two hundred horses, that is, the price of a single coupling which is then tirelessly compared—in nine distichs—to the joyful unions of the most diverse gods and heroes with their official wives. So it is that the second baby, Pratardana, comes into the world, though without—at this moment—any characterization by the poet. Punctual as destiny, Gālava appears forthwith:

"Let the girl be returned to me, and let the steeds remain with you, while I go elsewhere, O king, to seek the price of a marriage."[16]

From the next, the king of Bhoja, son of Uśīnara, also childless, the brahman-guardian tries to obtain the balance, the four hundred remaining horses, in exchange for the siring of two sons. The king would be amenable, but like the others he has only two hundred horses of the required species:

"I will thus beget only one son upon her, O brahman; I will follow the path that others have followed."[17]

The brahman, despite his bad luck, puts on a good face, delivers the girl to the king and, to await the event, enters the nearby forest where he devotes himself to austerities. The king seems to draw a good profit from his purchase—in the palace, in the gardens, on the mountains—and in this way a boy is born, Śibi, called upon in the words of the poet to become the best of kings. Gālava reclaims Mādhavī, a virgin for the third time, and sets out in quest for a fourth and last client. At this moment, the divine bird Garuḍa looms up before him once again and congratulates him on his success, which he believes to be complete. Gālava sets him straight: his capital still needs its last quarter to bear the required interest, and he has yet to find another buyer. "Do not make this endeavor," says the bird immediately: "it will bring you nothing more." And he recounts the early history of white horses with one black ear.[18]

The person responsible for their introduction into this world was Kānyakubja, who demanded a thousand of them from R̥cīka in return for his consent to a marriage with his daughter Satyavatī. R̥cīka's powers were beyond the ordinary: he proceeded to the abode of Varuṇa—a god with a traditional interest in the equine race—and there, at the "Hermitage of the Horses," Aśvatīrtha, he obtained a full cavalry entirely at his command. He presented it to his father-in-law. The latter celebrated a great sacrifice and, for fees, he gave the officiating priests six hundred of his marvelous horses: these are the horses which, having been sold and dispersed throughout the world, Gālava has already found and collected, in the lands of three kings, in groups of two hundred. As to the four hundred others, they died en route—although the text of the *Mahābhārata*, vague at this point, does not allow us to determine whether or not they drowned in a river of the Puñjab. The upshot is that Gālava now finds himself in possession of all the known examples of this species; no king, no market, will have any more. Garuḍa immediately extricates his friend from the difficulty raised for him by this revelation: let him seek out his *guru*, Viśvāmitra himself, present him with the six hundred horses, and offer him, as he has done with the three kings, the use of the girl as the equivalent of the remaining two hundred—a use limited, of course, to the engendering of a single son.

Gālava seems to have regained his courage, although it is true that the bird accompanies him to his master. With simplicity and firmness, he proposes the transaction:

"This girl," he says, "has already, from three rājarṣis, had three virtuous sons. Let her conceive a fourth by you, a single one, who will be the best of men. Admit then that the number of eight hundred horses is complete, and give me a receipt for the payment of my debt so that I may go to practice austerities freely."[19]

One could fear anything from a man like Viśvāmitra, who, in the dress of a brahman, conserves a kṣatriya identity. But this time, in the presence of this magnificent body, his kṣatriya past alone speaks forth in the voice of an imperious libido:

> "Why," he asked, "have you not brought me this girl sooner, Gālava? For myself, I would have engendered four sons, founders of lineages. I accept her from you, in order to have a single son by her. As to the horses, let them run freely near my hermitage."[20]

And the saintly man finds pleasure with Mādhavī, resulting in a son who receives the name Aṣṭaka. As soon as he is born, his father fills him with the *dharma* associated with *artha*, leaves him the six hundred marvelous horses, and sends him off as king to "a city equal to the city of Soma." Then, to his disciple, he returns the young mother, a virgin now for the fourth time, and resumes his life as a penitent in the forest. Gālava has nothing more to make from his lucrative ward. And so he tells her, handing over at the same time one of the keys—the trifunctional key—to the story:

> "To you is born a son who is a master of alms, a second who is a hero, another who is devoted to justice and truth, and yet another who is a sacrificer. Now go away, O beautiful girl, maid of slender waist. Thanks to these sons, you have saved us: not only your father, but also four kings, and myself."[21]

Gālava likewise dismisses his friend Garuḍa, gives Mādhavī back to Yayāti and, freed from all cares, finally is able to return to his beloved forest.[22]

So many adventures have not depreciated a girl who retains nothing from them to betray their effect. So her father resolves to give her a more durable husband by means of a *svayaṃvara*, a type of marriage in which it is the interested party herself who, from among the assembled suitors, chooses the master of her life. He drives her in a chariot, covered with garlands, to a place near a hermitage at the confluence of the Gaṅgā and the Yamunā. Pūru and Yadu accompany their sister (there is nothing about the three other brothers). At the place set for the ceremony, a great crowd throngs together—a crowd not just of men but of spirits of all sorts: Nāgas, Yakṣas, Gandharvas, even wild quadrupeds, birds, "inhabitants of the mountains, trees, and forests," not to mention all the great ṛṣis of the neighborhood. But at the moment of choice, she passes over all the candidates to select the forest—whose Sanskrit name, *vana*, is conveniently masculine—as her husband. She descends from her chariot, salutes her attendants, and disappears beneath the trees eager for the most severe austerities: living under a strict fast, she lightens her body with ascetic practices and begins to imitate the gazelle, living on green grass watered only by springs and torrents. And with her new congeners, the gazelles, as her companions, she wanders through the vast and tranquil forest, one that is destitute of lions, tigers, and conflagrations, and, through this mode of existence, amasses great merits.[23]

Henceforth, she would make only one more appearance among men, at the same time as her former "protector" Gālava:[24] this would be to help the four kings, her sons, to convince their dead and fallen grandfather, her father Yayāti, to agree to compensate for his fault by appropriating to himself their four varieties of merits. Into the pool of merits that will be made on that occasion, the gazelle-like penitent will turn over half of the profit from her own austerities; and Gālava, not a part of the family, will content himself with the discrete contribution of an eighth of his own.

2. Mādhavī, the Royal Virtues and the Salvation of the King

The western reader has perhaps felt uneasy at, or amused by, the matrimonial arrangements that yield the happy results just described. When we see this priest sell a girl's embraces to four kings in a row, calculating their pleasure by the price they can pay, retiring into the forest just for the time it will take, only to reappear and reclaim, for a new affair, one whom we hesitate to call his ward, we cannot help thinking of that controlled traffic, the traces of which are still, alas, to be found—despite the efforts of local authorities—in some of the big cities of our time. Even if, after each performance of her services, the young girl comes out intact, this does not seem to change—to make more acceptable, morally speaking—the well-known mechanism of the transaction. The western reader is mistaken: even from Gālava's point of view, the story is steeped in piety. Is it not to satisfy the demands of his spiritual master that this true ascetic, in a disinterested fashion, has accepted this singular means to acquire the eight hundred horses? Has not the girl's father himself delivered her to him, heroically perhaps, since he had no other way, direct or indirect, to come up with the considerable alms demanded of him? Does not the young girl herself, seeing her guardian in a quandary, propose—heroically also, perhaps—that he divide her worth in moon-colored horses by four and thus multiply by four the number of her partners? Finally, even if they are entirely provisional, are not these four marriages, under their set conditions, in fact true and honorable ones? To judge from the unmixed blessings which result from them and which are shared by all the parties concerned, it is at least evident that the gods have found nothing irregular in the procedure. But it is from the young girl's standpoint that the study of this series of incidents is, if one may say so, the most pregnant with revelations.

Mādhavī commits no sin: the choice of an ascetic life, of an animal life without animality, which she undertakes when she again finds herself free, is not an act of repentance, a sinner's expiation, but the belated realization of a vocation long thwarted—for approximately four years—by the execution of an urgent duty. The execution itself is apparently marred by no sexual emotions: rather she has acted out of pure *dharma* (virtue) with no trace of *kāma* (desire)—and the *artha* (profit) with which she has been concerned is an *artha* also pure in essence, intended for another person's advantage.

But what if these edifying motivations are no more than an Indian attempt to put a modest garment over a more ancient mechanism, one of a totally different order? For, as Gālava says in his farewell madrigal, Mādhavī has served many men at once. In fact, the brahman for whom she has obtained the six hundred moon-colored horses with one black ear apiece is perhaps not even the principal beneficiary. She has given sons to three different kings and to a former king turned brahman, none of whom had sons of their own nor any hope (this is at least certain for the first) of begetting them, were it not for her, this special girl, whom they have fortunately encountered; to the king her father she has given not only the grandson he desired, but four grandsons, who—even the brahman-kṣatriya's son—have become eminent kings in four lands and who, as small change for their grandfather, if one may say so, have excelled in the virtue typically corresponding to one of the three functions or parts of functions in which, taken together, their grandfather had excelled and which are necessary for a really great king. Through the medium of these grandsons, whose virtues have reconstituted the synthesis of merits, she has made her kingly father's posthumous restoration to his royal rank in heaven possible, and, in the finale, when her father's protestations multiply, by intervening with the gift of half her merits and thus reinforcing the gifts of the four kings issued from her, she at last removes his scruples. In short, this pious girl seems to hold within her some efficacious power which touches upon the very essence of royalty. The first of her temporary husbands does not fail to notice and remark upon it: seeing the auspicious marks she bears upon her body, he exclaims: "She is capable even of giving birth to a *cakravartin*"[25]—that rare variety of complete and perfect *homo regius* who would turn the wheel of the world and who customarily became a universal king until the Buddha opened up another option for his excellence. Transferred into the story of Yayāti, the real meaning behind this tableau of royal connections becomes apparent. Our preceding analyses have found in him a realization of the type of the "first king," on the same level as the Iranian king Yima: universal king, distributing parts of the earthly world to his five sons, the one elect and the four exiled; then, through the natures of his four grandsons, specialized kings, illustrating the system of the functions. Inserted between the two groups of figures, the sons and the grandsons, how are we to regard Mādhavī, sister of the first group, mother of the second, wife and virgin? What is the function of this short-term wife of several kings in succession for whom she does no more than assure the continuation of their royal lineages, above all producing in her royal sons, for the final benefit of her father, the complete set of canonical royal qualities?

Iran presents nothing comparable. There, as has been seen, the symbol for royal power is the victorious Glory, the *x*ᵛ*arənah*, efficacious on the three functional levels. At most, it may be noted that the old theme of the "victorious hero curled up in the stalk of a marine reed," well-known in India—which in Iran became the theme of the "royal *x*ᵛ*arənah* put on reserve at the base of a marine reed," and which appears at the mythical origin of the dynasty of the Kayanids—includes a curious feminine step in the role played by a "sister" after the elimination of her "brothers."[26] The scheme is this: someone has managed to make the *x^{v}arənah* pass from the reed into some milk, which he gives to his three sons to drink. The *x^{v}arənah* does not, however, penetrate into any of the sons but only into their sister, who has also presumably partaken of the milk. Through another man she conceives a son, and the *x^{v}arənah* passes on to him. She gives the boy as an adoptive son to the first Kavi. As a result, her son will be the second king of the new and still contested dynasty, and, from father to son, the *x^{v}arənah—kavaēm x^{v}arənah*, "the *x^{v}arənah* of the Kavis"—will accompany the line of the Kayanids, guaranteeing their power.[27] But even if this female giver of royalty and of royal posterity is to be aligned functionally, as I am led to believe she should be, with the Indian Mādhavī, the alteration that has resulted from notions proper to Zoroastrianism is so great that the comparison cannot be pressed farther.

3. Mādhavī's Name

At any rate, there is one striking difference between the Indian and Iranian narratives: the woman who bestows the Iranian royalty indeed receives the essence of royal power in a drink, but it is a drink of milk, of cow's milk. Mādhavī herself owes her name in the last analysis to the *madhu*, to the intoxication of the *madhu*, a fermented drink. Mādhavī is, in effect, the feminine of the adjective Mādhava, which classical Sanskrit substitutes for the Vedic adjective *mā́dhva* (feminine *mā́dhvī*),[28] a regular derivative from *mádhu*, whose semantic evolution is well-known: it is the Indian heir of the Indo-European word for hydromel, which, in India as in Greece, took on new meanings but in both cases referred to intoxication or to inebriating beverages. *Madhu* is also, in the epic, a masculine proper name, and several women bear the derived name Mādhavī in the sense of "belonging to the descent of Madhu, to the tribe of Madhu." But this is not the case here, since our heroine, Yayāti's daughter, did not descend from such a tribe or from anyone named Madhu. Her name must therefore be interpreted differently, more literally; and this can be done in only two possible ways, for Mādhavī, as an appellative, has two meanings, both when it occurs by itself and when it occurs in the compound *madhumādhavī*.

First meaning: (1) *mādhavī*, "springtime flower, Gaertnera Racemosa" (B[öhtlingk and] R[oth]): (2) *madhumādhavī*, "eine honigreiche Frühlingsblume oder eine bestimmte Blume" (BR), that which M[onier]- W[illiams] glosses: "any spring flower abounding in honey, or a particular species of flower, perhaps Gaertnera Racemosa (*Bhāg. Pur.*)."

Second meaning: (1) *mādhavī*, "ein berauschendes Getränk aus Honig" (BR), "an intoxicating drink" (M-W); (2) *madhumādhavī*, "ein bestimmtes berauschendes Getränk" (BR), "a kind of intoxicating drink (*Mbh.*)" (M-W). It is indeed the second meaning which is current in the *Mahābhārata*, as is certified by the explanations of the commentary. BR refers to two passages, one from III,288,16040:

> kathaṃ hi pītvā mādhvīkaṃ pītvā ca madhumādhavīm
> lobhaṃ sauvīrake kuryān nārī kācid iti smaret.

Let him reflect: how will a woman, after having drunk the intoxicating beverage called *mādhvīka* and after having drunk the intoxicating beverage called *madhumādhavī*, feel desire for sour gruel?

Here the commentary explains *mādhvīkam* by *madhupuṣpajam madyam*, "intoxicating drink produced from the *madhupuṣpa*," a flower which Roth, in BR, gives four interpretations according to the nomenclature of western botanists; and *madhumādhavīm* is explained by *kṣaudrajāṃ surām*, "alcohol produced from honey" [*kṣaudra*: (1) Michelia Campaka, (2) honey (BR)].

The other example is in the first book, in fact during the preliminaries of the Yayāti episode before his second encounter with the daughter of Kāvya Uśanas, the imperious Devayānī whom Yayāti soon will be constrained to marry. Devayānī is in the middle of an outing with her servant-princess Śarmiṣṭhā and their numerous female attendants. What are they doing? (I,81,3360–61)

> krīḍantyo 'bhiratāḥ sarvāḥ pibantyo madhumādhavīm
> khādantyo vividhān bhakṣyān vidaṃśantyaḥ phalāni ca.

(There they were), playing and amusing themselves all, drinking the *madhumādhavī*, eating morsels of various kinds, and biting into fruits.

This is the moment when king Yayāti, seeking for game and thirsting for water, *mṛgalipsuḥ* and *jalārthaḥ*, passes through these same places and perceives the host of pretty girls.

Here the commentary translates *madhumādhavīm* by *madhuvṛkṣajamādhavīm* (rightly giving to *mādhavī* the meaning of "intoxicating drink"), "inebriating drink produced by the *madhuvkṛṣa*" (= Bassa Latifolia, M-W, one of the four identifications also proposed for *madhupuṣpa*, BR, M-W).

There are, then, two choices—which ultimately come to the same thing—for the interpretation of the proper name Mādhavī: (1) either "intoxicating drink prepared with the help of a certain spring flower rich in honey"; (2) or else that flower itself, the raw material for the intoxicating drink. In both cases, actually or virtually, Mādhavī refers to that which makes for the intoxication from *madhu*. And that, at least in name, is what Mādhavī "is."

In the telling of the legend, this power has played no part: the intoxication which she inspires, when she appears, is only that of amorous desire, as much in the three kings to whom she is offered in succession as in the former king turned brahman who receives her as a fourth partner. But that does not prevent this figure so fully impregnated with royalty from still being called something like "the Intoxicating"—a trace, perhaps, of a more barbaric level of the tradition. We are far from milk, far from Iran.

4. Medb

But we are quite close to one of the strangest symbolic figures of the West, of the Celtic world, of the emerald isle, Ireland. We are, in fact, very close—both in name and, what is much more important, in function—to the famous queen, or queens, named *Medb*, in whom twentieth-century critics, with good reason but without a sufficient sense of nuance, have sought to recognize a personification of Irish royalty, of royal power defined by the requirement of three qualities. She too, under different and less virtuous conditions, is characterized by moving from one husband to the next, bringing royalty with her. And her name is transparent: it is **medhuā-*, feminine of the adjective **medhu̯o-*, from which is derived the Welsh *meddw*, "drunk." All are agreed on this etymology;[29] the only divergence is over the orientation, whether passive or active, of the proper meaning of this Gaelic adjective *medb* and of its feminine. The opinions are conveniently assembled and discussed on pages 112–14 of Josef Weisweiler's book

Heimat und Herrschaft, Wirkung und Ursprung eines irischen Mythos (1943). Heinrich Zimmer (1911), sticking to the sense of the Welsh word, translated Medb "die Betrunkene," "the Drunken One," and Rudolf Thurneysen (1930) leaned in the same direction, "eher die 'Trunkene' als die 'Berauschende,'" "rather the 'Drunk' than the 'Intoxicating'"; but Tomás ó Máille (1938) and Alwyn and Brinley Rees (1961) have preferred to understand the word as "the Intoxicating One," a meaning which Hessen has selected, with a question mark, in his *Irisches Lexicon* (volume 2, page 104): "*medb*, berauschend (?)." Weisweiler, page 114, has sought to reconcile the two interpretations by replacing them with a third, making *medb* no longer an adjective but a substantive, an "abstract formation" derived either from **medhu*, or from a verb **medhu̯ō* (Greek *μεθύω*), and signifying "Rausch, Trunkenheit," "drunkenness." In any case, says this author rightly, "there is obviously a connection between the intoxicating drink and the celebrated royal woman of Connaught".

The comparison of the functions and the comportments of the Irish Medb and the Indian Mādhavī confirms this etymology, whether in the sense of "drunkenness" or of "Intoxicating." But the comparison also discloses a parallelism of greater import between the father of Medb, the supreme king of Ireland, and the father of Mādhavī, the universal king Yayāti. This is quite an early reflection upon royalty, especially upon supreme royalty, which we see still mirrored, despite different evolutions, in the Irish and Indian legends.

5

EOCHAID FEIDLECH, HIS DAUGHTERS AND HIS SONS

1. Two Queens Named Medb

The most illustrious of the "queens Medb" is the one who comes from the province of Connaught, daughter of Ireland's supreme king Eochaid (or Eochu)[1] Feidlech. She is called "Medb of Cruachan" after the place of one of her residences. She plays a major role in *Táin Bó Cuailnge;* she is even at the bottom—as the cause—of the great conflict between her compatriots the men of Connaught and the men of Ulster, which is the subject of the epic. But that is only one episode among many others in her personal life: in fact, by her own decision or at the wish of her father, she had no less than four regular husbands, perhaps five, all of them kings.[2]

Her first husband was Conchobar, king of the Ulates; she left him "through pride of spirit," *tre uabar menman,* "in order to repair to Tara, where the (supreme) king of Ireland was," *co ndechaid chum Temrach in bail i raibe rí Erend,* that is, in order to return to her father's court.[3]

Her next suitor, Fidech son of Fiacc, was a native of Connaught (his name recalls Fidach, one of the departments, or "thirds," of this province), but he was eliminated by a rival, Tinde son of Conra Cass, also a man of Connaught. This is how it happened. Tinde was king of Connaught, but two princes had close ties to his kingship: Fidech son of Fiacc and Eochaid Dála (the latter belonging to another "third" of the province, that of the Fir Chraibe). Fidech went to Tara—the chief town in Mide, the Central Fifth, that of the supreme king—to establish his claim to the kingship, and there he asked the supreme king Eochaid Feidlech for the hand of his daughter Medb (*cur cuindidh Medb ar Eochaid Fedliuch*). Tinde caught wind of this scheme and set an ambush. The two troops met in the valley of the

Shannon, and one of Tinde's men killed Fidech. Medb's father then degraded Tinde (he imposed on him an "untruth of nobility," *anfir flátha*),[4] exiled him to the wilderness of Connaught, and "placed Medb at Cruachan in place of a king," *ocus cuiris Medhbh a n-inadh rígh a Cruachain;* but this was not enough to keep Medb and Tinde from meeting later and marrying, *co mba céledach.* The only effect of this maneuver by Medb's father was that the place named Cruachan became, for a time, the place where the assembly-festivals of Ireland were held, *conidh a Cruachain dognítea áenuig Érenn,* and the sons of the kings of Ireland took up the custom, before engaging in battle with the province of Conchobar (Ulster), "of being at Cruachan with Medb," *ocus nobittís mic reig Érend hi Cruachain ic Meidhbh.* Before her marriage to Tinde, from the time when she was "in the place of a king" at Cruachan, there was, in Connaught province, no shortage of suitors representing the four other "Fifths" of Ireland. As she herself tells at the beginning of the *Táin,* "messengers came on behalf of Find son of Rus Ruad, king of Leinster, to ask for me in marriage; on behalf of Cairpri Nia Fer son of Rus Ruad, king of Tara; of Conchobar son of Fachtna Fathach, king of Ulster; and of Eochaid Bec [a kinglet of Munster]; and I did not go there." This reappearance of Conchobar has surprised some commentators, as has another more lively story which tells how, when Medb's father had brought his daughter to the festivals at Tara, Conchobar stayed behind after the completion of the games, lay in wait for Medb while she went to bathe herself in the river Boyne, and raped her. But did he not have an old account to settle with her?[5]

Tinde was killed opportunely in the battle that followed, and it was the second prince with close ties to this king—Eochaid Dála—who, not without a fight, brought Medb back safe and sound to her kingdom, together with the troops which had accompanied her. As a result, Eochaid Dála became king; more exactly, he was designated by the notables as king of Connaught, "Medb having consented to it on the condition that she would become his spouse," *do déoin Medba dia mbeth na chele dhi fen.* But this condition itself depended on another: not being herself the suitor, Medb reserved the right to accept or refuse. Now, it was her practice to refuse any partner who "was not without jealousy, without fear, and with avarice, for it was a *geis*—an interdiction under magical sanction—that she would accept as a husband only a man who combined these three qualities," *cen étt cen omun cen neoith do beth ann, uair ba ges disi beth ac ceili a mbeitís na trée sin.* Eochaid Dála presumably took on the triple obligation, or made the triple demonstration which it required, for "he became king in consequence of this, *doríghad Eochaid trit sin,* and was then for a time at Cruachan as the spouse of Medb, *ana chele icc Meidb.*"[6]

But already the fourth husband had appeared, he who would have the honor of appearing in the *Táin.* At that time, in Connaught, a young boy called Ailill, son of Rus Ruad, king of Leinster, was being raised. His mother was a native of Connaught, so that the people of this province regarded him as one of their own. Moreover, "never were jealousy nor fear found in his heart," *ocus dano na frith et no omun inna chridiu,* an indication that he fulfilled at least two-thirds of Medb's standard requirements. She went to Leinster to take him with her to Connaught, and there, very quickly, he became an accomplished warrior. "And Medb loved him for his qualities and he was united with her and became her husband in place of Eochaid Dála." The latter made the mistake of showing his jealousy, *cur étluighi Eochaid,* which eliminated him once and for all. The clans interfered, but Medb held firm "because she preferred Ailill to Eochaid." There was a battle in which Ailill killed his predecessor; and then he became king of Connaught "with Medb's consent, so that he was the king of this province on two important occasions: at the coronation of Etarscéle, and at the beginning of the *Táin Bó Cuailnge,*" Medb gave him three sons, the three named "Maine."[7]

There is sometimes a question of a fifth husband, supposedly the progenitor, with Medb, of a subordinate clan widely scattered over Ireland, that of the Conmaicne. This Fergus was celebrated for the size of his penis.[8] The canonical list does not mention this last affair, but the rich get richer, and Medb herself had good reasons for saying, at the beginning of the *Táin*: "I have never been without one man near me in the shadow of another," *na raba-sa riam cen fer ar scáth araile ocum.*[9]

The second Medb, Medb Lethderg, daughter of Conán Cualann, was queen of Leinster, *rígain do Laignib.*[10] It is said of her that she gave two children to king Cú Corb—a descendant of Rus Ruad, one of the suitors, then a father-in-law of Medb of Cruachan—but that when Cú Corb was killed by Feidlimid Rechtaid, son of Tuathal Techtmhar, king of Ireland, she became the wife of the victor, who was famous above all as the father of Conn Cétcathach, "Conn of a hundred battles." "Truly great was the force and power of this Medb over the men of Ireland," one text says, "for she tolerated no king at Tara unless he took her as his wife, *roba mor tra nert ocus cumachta Meidhbha insin for firu Erenn, air isi na leigedh rí a Temair gan a beth feir aigi na mnái;* and it is for her that the royal *rath* (a kind of enclosure), the Rath Medba, was constructed near Tara, and there she made a building where the kings and the masters of all arts, *righa ocus ollamuin gacha dana*, came together."

She did not limit herself to these two husbands, but, at least for her regular partners, she did not seem to look beyond the dynasty. After Feidlimid, father of Conn, she married Art, son of Conn, and after him Cormac, son of Art. And, as one text specifies, it was this marriage, and it alone—not heredity—which allowed Cormac to assume royalty. "Cormac grandson of Conn," a text says, "lived at Kells before assuming the royalty of Ireland after the death of his father (Art). Medb Lethderg of Leinster had been the wife of Art and, after the latter's death, she took the royalty, *ocus arrobert side in rige iar n-ecaib Airt*."[11] A poem is specific on this point:

> The Leinstermen of the spears made over the sovereignty to the son of the king of Eire;
> not until Meadhbh [Medb] was united to the son [of the king of Ireland, i.e. of Cathaoir Mor] did Cormac become king of Eire.[12]

2. Medb, Sovereignty, and the Royal Virtues

The existence of two identically named doublets, one in the legends of Connaught, the other in the legends of Leinster, both diversely connected with the central Fifth, guarantees that the "Medb type" is indeed a variety of those feminine personifications of power, of *flaith*, of which Ireland presents other examples—sometimes under the simple name Flaith—and which have prospered down to the French and English romances of the Middle Ages. The most famous examples are found in the two stories of Niall and Lugaid Láigde. I mention them because they present a type of personification that is ruder than the type we see in Medb and, despite what has been said, not exactly its duplicate.

In their youth, Niall and his four half-brothers, Brian, Fiachra, Ailill, and Fergus, having received weapons, went to try them out in the hunt. They lost their way and lit a great fire to cook the game they had killed. As they had nothing to drink, the last brother went in search of a water supply. He came before a spring guarded by an old sorceress who would not allow him to draw from it unless he gave her a kiss. He refused and came back with his bucket empty. One after another, the three intermediary brothers had the same experience, with the only exception that one, Fiachra, deigned to graze the woman with his lips, in reward for which she promised him "a brief contact with Tara," announcing to him thereby that only two of his descendants would become kings. When it came to the youngest, Niall's turn, he was less fastidious: he clasped the old woman and covered her with kisses. Presumably he closed his eyes for, when he looked, he saw himself in the grip of the most beautiful woman in the world. "Who are you?" he asked. "King of Tara," she answered—thus saluting him as "supreme king" —"I am Sovereignty and your descendants will be above every clan." And, sending him back toward his brothers, she recommended to him that he not allow them to drink before they had recognized his rights and his superiority.[13]

Very close to this story, with a supplement, is the story of the five sons of king Dáire.[14]

It had been foretold to Dáire that a "son of Dáire," named "Lugaid," would attain the kingship of Ireland. For more assurance, to all the boys who were born to him he gave the same name, Lugaid. One day, at Teltown—a place where there were seasonal feasts and games—his sons were set to participate in a horserace, and there a druid specified to Dáire that his heir would be the one who succeeded in catching a fawn with a golden fleece who would enter the assembly. The fawn indeed appeared and, while it was being pursued, a magical mist separated the five brothers from all the other hunters. It was Lugaid Láigde who caught the animal. Then a great snow began to fall and one of the brothers set off in search of shelter. He was able to find a house with a great fire, food and ale, silver dishes, a bronze bed and a horrible sorceress. This latter offered the boy a bed for the night on the condition that she herself would share intimately in his repose. He refused, and she declared to him that in so doing he had just deprived himself of Sovereignty. The other brothers then came one after another to present themselves at the same house, but the sorceress asked nothing from them—until, last of all, came Lugaid Láigde who, with astonishment, saw the old body, under his embrace, become radiant like the rising sun in the month of May and fragrant like a beautiful garden. As he clasped her, she said to him: "Happy is your journey, for I am Sovereignty,[14] and you shall attain the sovereignty over all of Ireland."[15]

The story is interesting because it brings into play, in parallel—one confirming the other—two symbols or signs of sovereignty, the woman and the fawn, both of them encountered in the woods.[16]

Queen Medb, who conceals her beauty under no mask and lays no traps for the pretenders to royalty save her charms, symbolizes another aspect of power; she is no longer linked solely to a sometimes fortuitous conquest of royalty, but to a regular, controlled conquest and, above all, to the practice of royalty. It is she who defines royalty and rigorously sets its "moral" conditions. With her, it is no longer a question of chance, of boldness, of gallantry, but of merits. She does not satisfy herself with one partner but multiplies them, shamelessly delights in making them vie with each other under the pretext of assessing their qualities.

It may well have been the spectacle, the experience—unceasingly renewed—of the instability of the throne that oriented this figure, more and more, it would seem, toward a career of cynicism and debauchery. In the same way another experience, that of the waves of blood which flowed in the princely contests, appears to have earned for the other Medb, Medb of Leinster, her qualification *Leth-derg*, "of the red side" or "of the red half." That experience may also explain the epithet applied to the maidservant of Medb of Connaught's mother, passed on afterward to Medb's mother herself, Cruachu or Crochen *Chró-derg*, "of red skin," or "red blood."[17] So, too, the difficulties which marked the beginnings of the finest reigns gave rise—as the texts relating to Niall say quite plainly[18]—to the theme of the splendid woman who first presents herself under the guise of a horrible hag.

The close tie of the queens Medb with the practice of, and the "moral" conditions for, royalty follows from the three challenges which the more famous of the two threw out to anyone who aspired to become her husband, that is, to become king. These were mentioned above: the chosen one had to be, had to prove himself to be, and had to continue to be "without jealousy, without fear, and without avarice." In 1941, at the end of my first *Jupiter Mars Quirinus*, I summarily proposed that this formula be understood as a psychological, almost Platonic expression of the structure of the three functions.[19] At the beginning of the *Táin Bó Cuailnge*, addressing her consort Ailill, the interested party herself enlarges upon the formula in very much the same way, except that she brings the most elevated term of the triad, jealousy, down to her own personal problems as a wife:

"... for it is I," she says, "who exacted a singular bride-gift, such as no woman before had ever required of a man of the men of Ireland, namely, a husband without avarice, without jealousy, without fear.

For should he be avaricious, the man with whom I should live, we were ill-matched together, inasmuch as I am great in largess and gift-giving, and it would be a disgrace for my husband if I should be superior to him in the matter of favors, and for it to be said that I was superior in wealth and treasures to him, while no disgrace would it be if one were as great as the other.

Were my husband a coward, it would be equally unfit for us to be mated, for I by myself and alone brave battles and fights and combats, and it would be a reproach for my husband should his wife be more courageous than he, while there would be no reproach for our being equally brave, both of us brave.

Should he be jealous, the husband with whom I should live, that too would not suit me, for there never was a time I had not near me one man in the shadow of another.

Yet, I have found such a man: it is you, Ailill son of Rus Ruad of Leinster. You were not avaricious, you were not jealous, you were not a coward."[20]

In the practice of royal power, "jealousy" is a little more than this coquettish wife of so many kings has indicated here; or rather, the symbol calls for interpretation: to be jealous, to have a morbid fear of rivals, checks, and counterchecks, such are the spurs to tyranny in all its aspects, judicial as well as political. With this reservation, the justifications that Medb gives for her demands, speaking as a wife and not simply allegorically, are pertinent. They have been treated excellently by Alwyn and Brinley Rees in their *Celtic Heritage*.

The three qualities essential to a king are defined in a negative way in Queen Medb's requirements in a husband. He must be "without jealousy, without fear, and without niggardliness." Jealousy would be a fatal weakness in a judge, as would fear in a warrior and niggardliness in a farmer. The higher the status, the more exacting are the standards that go with it, and it is noteworthy that the most reprehensible sin in each class is to indulge in the foibles of the next class below it. Meanness may be excused in a serf, but it is the denial of the farmer's vocation; fear is not incompatible with the peaceful role of the farmer, but it is the warrior's greatest disgrace; jealousy, as we have seen, is a trait of the warrior's character, the correlative of his virtue, but it can undermine the impartiality required in a judge. A king must have the virtues of all the functions without their weaknesses.[21]

Such was the mission of "Queen Medb," of Royalty personified: to see to it that the king, each new king, would have the assortment of qualities which had been demonstrated by a very early analysis—already present in the Indo-European tradition—to be an absolute necessity for the equilibrium of a society and the success of a reign; and also, once those qualities were ascertained in a prince, to give him the throne. Moreover, she herself, before formulating and expounding these three conditions at the beginning of the *Táin*, took care to claim credit for the corresponding qualities herself:

> . . . I was the most noble and the most distinguished (of my father's six daughters): I was the best of them in kindness and generosity (*bam-sa ferr im rath ocus tidnacul díb*): I was the best among them in battle, combat, and fighting (*bam-sa ferr im chath ocus comrac ocus comluid díb*). . . .[22]

She goes on, complacently, to add that the young nobles who formed her normal retinue numbered five hundred. Thus, to generosity and bravery, she added implicitly, as her third and highest advantage, her power to maintain about her in an orderly fashion—without jealousy!—a most illustrious outfit of courtiers.

Celticists have asked themselves how the essence of royalty came to be personified under a name which, drawn from that of the Indo-European mead, essentially expresses the power of intoxication.[23] They have collected texts in which the drink is highlighted in connection with either the practice or the acquisition or the exaltation of royal power. Few of these texts are really conclusive. For instance, an argument cannot be drawn from the metered praises of a king of Leinster:

> The sovereignty (*ind flaith*) is his heritage. . . . At the beer-drinking bout (*oc*

cormaim) poems are recited.... The harmonious songs of bards make the name of Aed resound through the drinks of beer (*tri laith-linni*).

What could be more natural than for the king to be celebrated at the banquets he offers? More interesting is the obligation upon the king to offer them. A juridical text, enumerating the four activities of the king, begins with this obligation:

to drink beer (*do ól corma*) on Sundays, for there is no regular sovereign (*flaith techta*) who does not promise beer (*laith*) every Sunday.[24]

But that could still rest upon the assonance between the names for "power" (*flaith*) and "beer" ((*f*)*laith*).[25] The most noteworthy arguments are furnished by the fairly numerous legends which make the acquisition of royalty depend upon a certain drink, for instance the *derg-flaith*, "red beer" or "red sovereignty," which the personified Sovereignty of Ireland, in a dream, pours out for king Conn; or the "old beer" and the automatic drinking horns in the story of Lugaid Láigde; or the spring water which the sorceress Sovereignty allows to be drunk only in exchange for a kiss and which is at least the prelude to less harmless beverages, since the old woman turned young says to Niall: "May the drink (*linn*) that will flow from the royal horn be for you: it will be mead, it will be honey, it will be strong beer!" After citing these examples and several others, Josef Weisweiler adds the following, concerning one of the two Medbs directly:

It is told of Medb of Cruachan that she intoxicated heroes to obtain their cooperation in the struggle against her enemies. The tragic duel between Fer Diad and his brother-in-arms Cúchulainn took place only because Medb made Fer Diad swallow, until he became drunk, "an intoxicating beverage, good, sweet to drink." She had already resorted to the same means in order to arm, put at her service, and send to his death Fer Báeth, foster brother of Cúchulainn, and Lárine mac Nois. There is obviously a connection between the intoxicating drink and the celebrated royal woman of Connaught.[26]

As to Medb of Leinster, she is called "daughter of Conán of Cuala" (*ingen Chonain Cualann*); now a medieval poet has written, evidently alluding to a tradition that was well understood in his time:

niba ri ar an Erind, mani toro coirm Cualand.

He will not be king over Ireland, unless the beer of Cuala should come to him.[27]

Thus the names for the two Medbs are justified, born perhaps from special royal rites which it would be as easy to imagine as it would be vain.

3. Medb and Mādhavī

We are now able to return to the Indian Mādhavī, daughter of the universal king Yayāti, wife and mother of multiple kings at an accelerated pace. If the account we have of her quadruple performance is fraught with pious thoughts and unfolded in conformity with the most respectable laws, both religious and civil, of brahmanic society, the story of the Irish Medb makes it likely that an extremely ancient notion has been conserved under this guise—proudly taking its place between the two other episodes in Yayāti's career. Let us put it bluntly: beyond the Indo-Iranian stage assured for the first and third episodes, this whole story continues to cast in poetic images an Indo-European theory of the nature, the chances, the risks of royalty and, above all, the qualities it requires. In particular, the trifunctional demands imposed by Medb upon all her royal husbands on the one hand, and the coherent trifunctional partnership formed by the royal sons of Mādhavī on the other, are two expressions of the analysis of these qualities in the most general framework of the Indo-European ideology.[28] And the synthesis is no less strongly delineated than the analysis: it is evident in the three demands of Medb, which are indissociable; and it is no less evident in the story of the sons of Mādhavī, who, although ruling over diverse lands, find themselves, against every custom and expectation, offering a common royal sacrifice on the very day that their own grandfather, formerly omnivalent in merits himself, needs them to reunite their merits and thus to recompose the complete trifunctional equipment he has lost.[29]

Behind Medb, behind both Medbs, there is a father, just as there is one behind Mādhavī: it is the father who gives Medb of Cruachan in marriage, at least to several of her husbands, and initially to the first, Conchobar, as part of the compensation for the wrong he had done him; it is the father of Medb of Leinster who disposes of the beer of sovereignty which appears to be inseparable from his daughter. And the supreme king of Tara is, by definition, the king of the "central Fifth" like Yayāti. Although the latter is in a position to divide up the surrounding lands between his five sons, he is properly the king of the good central land, since that is the "Fifth" which he reserves for the son whom he will make his successor.

Other features of the Indian legend are better explained in the light of the Irish phantasmagoria on sovereignty. Richer and more varied, this Irish tradition, in addition to Medb, presents Flaith, the beautiful young woman disguised as an old sorceress, and also the fawn which doubles for her in the story of Lugaid Láigde. It will be recalled that after her fourth child is born, Mādhavī, called upon to "make an end of it" in a socially dazzling way, that is, to marry herself "for good" to a decent prince, chooses at the height of the ceremony to unite herself not to a man but to the forest (*vana* being masculine), and that she in fact withdraws into the woods to devote herself to asceticism. Up to this point there is nothing noteworthy other than her decision to conserve from now on, away from all jeopardy, a virginity four times gambled. But the form of her asceticism, of her mystical marriage, is singular: she takes on the mode of life, the food, the lightness of a large *mr̥ga*, that is to say, of a gazelle or some animal of the same type, and it is presumably as such that she appears to her father the king and her four royal sons at that sublime reckoning of accounts which, in the providential plan whose existence we must take for granted, seems to be her final raison d'être.[30] We are truly close to Lugaid's fawn: here the two representations, the Beauty and the Beast, are united.

Just as the Irish have, on the one hand, the more concrete and more human Medb, a woman and a queen, and, on the other, the royal Power personified, Flaith, who, in a slightly different fashion, governs the rhythm of realms but, despite her technique of appearing at first repulsive and then seductive, remains more abstract, so in India the figure of Mādhavī is similarly akin, although without duplicating her, to the more abstract Śrī-Lakṣmī, "Prosperity," especially royal prosperity. Śrī-Lakṣmī has been rightly compared, by Alexander H. Krappe, Ananda Coomaraswamy, and Alwyn and Brinley Rees, to the Irish Flaith.[31] The acquisition of Śrī is also sometimes conceived of as a marriage. Śrī is the wife of Indra, seeks his protection, offers him the soma drink which she has caused to ferment by mastication, following an archaic technique. She is, like Flaith, an inconstant beauty, who, in an important episode of the *Mahābhārata*, passes from the demons to the gods, namely to the king of the gods, Indra.[32] At the time of the royal enthronement ceremony itself, she is connected with a rite which symbolizes that the *śrī*, the good fortune, of the king about to be consecrated, has escaped from him in its trifunctional component parts, later to be restored to him by a group of his queens.[33]

Finally, while Medb of Connaught scoffs at what will be said of her, parades her favors from one whim to the next, and expounds with complete frankness the theory behind her infidelities,[34] the pious Mādhavī passes from royal bed to royal bed out of duty and without licentiousness. But the fact is there, objectively, that she multiplies these experiences. Mādhavī's originality, of little importance for the two Medbs, is that she associates virginity with the intensive practice of remunerated unions, of temporary marriages by sale: four times she recovers her integrity, and it is with the obvious mark of innocence that she goes off as a gazelle in the forest of her choice.

Wide and deep as these correspondences are, they do not, of course, preclude considerable divergences, but the latter can in large part be accounted for by the different "ideological fields" of Ireland and India.

Thus, as we have seen, Mādhavī no longer bears any mark of drunkenness except in her name[35] and in the overwhelming desires which she arouses in all the kings to whom she is offered, whereas Medb, both Medbs, seem to be ritually associated with the practice of taking intoxicating drinks.[36] This is in conformity with the moral emphasis of the two societies: the Irish are always engaged in enormous drinking bouts, catalysts for acts of violence but also for exploits inconceivable in brahmanic India, which is hostile to the *surā*, to alcohol, and even—despite the example of the Vedic Indra—to the ritual abuse of the *soma*.

In the action of the two heroines, Ireland has highlighted the multiplicity of the husbands of Medb, making but few references to the offspring which result from these unions, a focus which accentuates the licentious aspect of her conduct. India, on the contrary, places the accent on the multiple sons of Mādhavī, on her efficacy as a mother, and also, with regard to Yayāti, on her daughterly piety. The only notes of voluptuousness in the account of her four unions are attributed to the royal buyers, not to Mādhavī, the innocent merchandise. In return, the western reader can boast that Medb, independent and proud, receives no fee for her services, while those of Mādhavī are paid for, although at a uniform rate—and not, of course, to her but to her rightful protector, who watches less over her than over the exactitude of the transactions.

Then too, the point at which Medb and Mādhavī apply that "royal virtue" which they have within them is not the same. Each of the Medbs, through her marriage, veritably creates kings in one of the provinces of the isle or, rather, at Tara, thus qualifying for the royalty of that province—or for the supreme royalty—men who, without her, would not have obtained such rank. Mādhavī, the good and beautiful dam, is commended, one after another, to three ruling kings and to a king emeritus, so that she may give them pleasure, certainly, but above all so that she may bear each a son who will become a king naturally, without her having to intervene.

In Mādhavī, India presents no equivalent to the rivalries, the conflicts sometimes ending in dispossessions, which occur again and again around the two Medbs—and, perhaps by way of compensation, this makes Mādhavī's sphere of action much larger. However fickle her Irish counterparts, they each operate in a single place and one of them, Medb of Leinster, in a single dynasty. Neither of the two Medbs, as long as her previous husband remains a king, tours the other royal beds of the island, and it is precisely because their virtue, if one can call it that, operates in a fixed and determined spot that all the rivalries, all the "palace revolutions," take place. On the contrary, Mādhavī's four clients are geographically and politically dispersed, and there is no risk of their succeeding each other on a single throne; thus, between them, there is neither competition nor jealousy. Two formulations make it clear that the successive embraces of the queen and the princess are different not in nature but in circumstances and consequences. Medb, for her part, says to one of her royal partners (the fourth): "There never was a time when I had not near me one man in the shadow of another," meaning that for the single throne with which she is concerned, there will always be a pretender ready to take the occupant's place;[37] on Mādhavī's part, one of her royal partners says to her venerable protector: "I will thus beget only one son upon her, I will tread in my turn the path that others have trod," showing thereby that, in these successive acts of common exploitation, none of the participants holds any threat for the others.[38]

On all these divergent points, one may be inclined to think that the Celts have retained in greater purity a system of concepts and images which, in the Indian version, is presented only as it has been domesticated by the brahmans, who were better casuists and more uncompromising moralists than the Druids.

Thus we are borne by the comparison well beyond Iran in space, and farther back than the second millennium B.C. in time. Between the conservative Ireland of the early middle ages and the conservative India of the epic, a direct, solid correspondence emerges here, to which a few scraps from Iran, though much paler and more distorted, may be added, recomposing the picture of a special accord between the extreme east and the extreme west of the Indo-European domain that has been exemplified so frequently. The correspondence, moreover, relates to the status of the **rēg-*, that is, to a figure whose name is attested only in the same two groups of societies.[39] To be sure, one must not draw hasty conclusions from this limitation, perhaps a provisional one,[40] but what we have just glimpsed is certainly important, and can perhaps be formulated briefly by reference to the episodes that make up the full-length saga of Yayāti.

1. In the first episode, we are struck by the coincidence of the division of Ireland into five Fifths—a central one, that of the supreme king, and four peripheral ones—with the Indian king's distribution of the lands among his five sons, establishing his heir at the center, exiling the four others to the circumference (and probably, in Vedic times, to the four quarters of the circumference). Although this "pattern," based on the cardinal points, is found throughout the world, it is remarkable that, among Indo-European societies, only the Irish and the Indians (and probably the most ancient Iranians too) preferred it to tripartite patterns.[41]

2. In the second episode, there is a striking correspondence between the Irish Medb and Mādhavī, daughter of Yayāti, both successive wives of several kings and probable incarnations of royal power in the forms and within the limitations which have been specified.

3. Again in the second episode but with its continuation in the third, we note the insertion of the ideological structure of the three functions into the activities of both heroines: in Medb, through the qualities which she demands in her husbands (absence of avarice, absence of fear, absence of jealousy); in Mādhavī, through the excellences which are distributed naturally among her offspring (generous use of riches, valor in battle, liturgical exactitude, veracity).

4. Eochaid, His Sons, and His Daughter Clothru

To these concordances is added another, more important, perhaps, since it proves that the full extent of the saga of Yayāti—with its plan, a diptych presenting the sons on the one hand, the daughter and her sons on the other—is ancient, pre-Indian. For it is indeed a diptych, despite the three-part analysis we have just made of it. In the first episode, the universal king is involved only with his five sons, and, with one exception, it is a bad relationship: the sons fail to submit, or to show respect, to their royal father, the royal father then deprives the ungrateful or rebellious sons, as well as their descendents, of their natural heritage, and establishes, to their detriment and in favor of a single son who has shown himself dutiful, a revised order of succession to the central throne. In the second episode and in the third which is its sequel, the sons hardly appear and have no real roles; the protagonists are now the king's daughter and the grandsons she gives him, and all—they and she alike—manifest a vivid, total devotion to the king, their father and grandfather.

Now Medb occupies a homologous place in the total legend of her father Eochaid which, with the exception of an episode of sin and redemption, hardly conceivable in the ideology of Ireland, follows the same plan, gives the same lesson as that of Yayāti. Eochaid, supreme king of Ireland, appears first with his sons, then with his daughters and principally with Medb, in antithetical situations. The text which informs us most systematically about Medb's marriages and which was summarized earlier,[42] the *Cath Boinde*, in fact opens, after the inevitable biblical reference, with a double tableau:

A king took kingship over Ireland once on a time: Eochaid Feidleach, the son of Finn, the son of Rogen Ruad, son of Easamain Eamna [. . .]. He was called Eochaid Feidleach because he was *feidil*, that is to say, just toward all.[43]

1. He had four sons: [first] the three Findeamna [*e(a)mna*, plural of *e(a)main*, "twin":[44] the "Finn triplets"], and they were born of one birth, Breas, Nar, and Lothar were their names. It is they who, in their own sister, engendered Lugaid-of-the-three-red-stripes [*Lugaid tri* (*sic*) *riab n-derg*] the night before they gave battle to their father, at Druimcriad. The three of them fell there by the hand of Eochaid Feidleach, and Eochaid Feidleach solemnly decided [on this occasion] that no son should ever rule Ireland [immediately] after his father—that which verified itself.[45] The [fourth] son of Eochaid Feidleach was Conall Anglondach,[46] who indeed did not become supreme king and from whom descend the Conailli, in the land of the men of Breagh.

As far as I know, no text explains the cause of the sons' coalition, but the battle fought by the sons against their father and lost by them is mentioned with more detail in other texts. Thus in an "explanation of place names" (*Dindšenchas*) under the heading of the place called Druim Criach:

Druim nAirthir ["Ridge of the east"] was the name at first, till the three Find-emna gave battle to their father there, even to Eochaid Feidleach, king of Ireland. Bres and Nar and Lothar were their names. . . . They marched through the north of Ireland over Febal and over Ess Rúaid, and crossed [the rivers] Dub and Drobáis and Dall and Sligech, and over Senchorann and Segais and Mag Luirg and Mag nAi and Mag Cruachan, and there their sister Clothru sought them, and wept to them, and kissed them. And she said: "I am troubled at being childless," and she entreated them to lie with her. And thence was born Lugaid Red-stripes [*Lugaid Riab ndearg*], the son of the three Find-emna. This was done that they might not get "truth of battle" [?] from their father.

Thereafter they marched from Cruachan over Áth Luain through Meath, over Áth Féne and Findglais and Glais Tarsna and Glais Cruind and Druim nAirthir.

Thrice three thousand were then with Eochaid, and he ordered a fast against his sons to overthrow them, or to make them grant him a month's truce from battle. Nothing, however, was given him save battle on the following day. So then Eochaid cursed his sons and said, "Let them be like their names" [Noise and Shame and Trough]. And he delivered battle [to his sons and their troops], and crushed seven thousand of them; and the sons were routed with only thrice nine men in their company, to wit, nine with Nar, who reached Tír ind Náir in Umall, and there he fell at Liath na cor;

and nine others with Bres at Dún Bres by Loch Orsben, and there he fell; and nine others with Lothar over Áth Lúain, and there he fell and, like his brothers, was beheaded.

Then before nightfall their three heads came to Druim Criaich, and there Eochaid uttered the word, that from that time forward no son should ever take the lordship of Tara after his father unless some one came between them.[47]

The treatise on the "Fitness of Words," *Cóir anman*, also proposes to connect Eochaid's epithet, Feidlech, with this painful family conflict: the word, it is claimed, is contracted from *fedil-uch*, "long sigh," because "after his sons had been killed at the battle of Druim Críad, the pain never left his heart until he died."[48] This etymology, certainly false, attests at least to the importance of the episode in the traditions about this king.

After this destruction of the rebellious sons, the *Cath Bóinde* then passes, without transition, to Eochaid's daughters:

2. That king, Eochaid Feidlech, had a great family, namely:

(a) Eile, daughter of Eochaid, wife of Fergal mac Magach; from her Bri Eili in Leinster takes its name; after Fergal she was wife to Sraibgend mac Niuil of the tribe of the Erna, and she bore him a son, Mata the son of Sraibgend, the father of Ailill mac Mata;

(b) Mumain Etanchaithrech, daughter of Eochaid Feidlech, wife of Conchobar son of Fachtna Fathach,[49] the mother of Glaisne Conchobar's son;

(c) Eithne, daughter of Eochaid Feidlech, another wife of the same Conchobar, mother of Furboide Conchobar's son [. . .];

(d) Clothra [= Clothru], daughter of Eochaid Feidlech, mother of Cormac Conloinges, Conchobar's son [. . .];

(e) Deirbriu, daughter of Eochaid Feidlech, from whom were named the "pigs of Deirbriu" [*muca Deirbrend*];

(f) Mea[d]b [that is, Medb] of Cruachan, daughter of Eochaid Feidlech, another of Conchobar's wives, mother of Amalgad, Conchobar's son, so that Conchobar was Medb's first husband [*conad he Concobar cet fear Meadba*], but Medb forsook Conchobar through pride of mind, and went [back] to Tara, where the supreme king of Ireland was.

The reasons that the supreme king [of Ireland] gave these daughters to Conchobar was that it was by Eochaid Feidlech that Fachtna Fathach [Conchobar's father] had fallen in the battle of Lottir-ruad in the Corann, so that it was as his eric [compensation] these were given to him, together with forcible seizure of the kingship of Ulster, over the children of the Clan

Rudraidhe; and the first cause of the stirring up of the Táin Bó Cuailnge ["the Cattle-raid of Cuailnge"] was the abandonment of Conchobar by Medb against his will.[50]

Thus, like Yayāti, Eochaid is maltreated by his sons (in this text, by all but the fourth). He curses them and, still more unfortunate than Yayāti, has to fight them; and, instead of having to exile them by royal command, he makes them flee in three directions and sees them perish in their flight. Moreover, as Mādhavī does for Yayāti, his daughters make him happy in various ways. They are obedient girls. He uses several of them to pay compensation and thus avoid a showdown with Conchobar.[51] One of them, in particular, gives him a very odd grandson, Lugaid, whose body—thanks to his three fathers—is divided in three by circular red stripes; and, by so doing, she saves her father. Another daughter, the last and the most fully described, Medb, performs through her marriages, as we have seen, a role in the presentation and the transfer of royalty. Finally, at the conclusion of his conflict with his sons, Eochaid makes a general decision, but one whose primary effect is upon the succession of his own throne—a decision different from that one made by Yayāti in like circumstances, more serious but with the same meaning: Yayāti limits himself to removing his four eldest sons from the universal kingship, that with the central seat, which he transmits to his youngest; Eochaid, on the other hand, forever prohibits any son of a supreme king from succeeding directly, without an interim reign, to the supreme kingship of Ireland.

The role of Eochaid's daughters is particularly interesting. Most of them have been given as wives to Conchobar, like Medb, and in this capacity seem to be doublets for her. But one of them, it will be recalled, intervenes in an original way: under a specious pretext, she offers herself to the concupiscence of her brothers before they begin their unfilial battle against their father. One of the texts which has just been cited explains this action all too briefly, but in the right direction: the girl acts out of daughterly devotion, sacrifices herself in three incestuous unions in order to mystically and perhaps physically weaken her brothers, to put them at a disadvantage against their father. Another text, the *Aided Medba* of the Book of Leinster, which Françoise Le Roux has recently made available as additional documentation in this area, is more explicit.[52] The text also has the advantage of making it clear that Clothru is a double, or a duplication, of Medb: she is called "Clothru of Cruachan," as Medb is "Medb of Cruachan," and it is said that she was in fact queen of this place before Medb. And here we find, fully unveiled, the plan which Clothru conceives: when her three brothers undertake to dethrone their father, she at first tries to dissuade them. Unsuccessful, she uses the following bold scheme: "Come to me," she says, "in order to know whether I will have a descent, for it is the hour and the moment of conception!" And that is what they do. They approach her in succession, and she conceives a son, Lugaid of the Red Stripes, son of the three Findemna. Then she says to them: "Now you will not go forth against your father. You have committed enough evil by uniting with your sister. That will do: do not fight against your father." And so it is, the text of the *Aided Medba* concludes, that she prevents them from being triumphant in the upcoming battle. Mme Le Roux comments aptly: "The most likely interpretation is that Clothru paralyzes her brothers or deprives them of their martial vigor, all the while assuring her father of a male descendant"—a very necessary male descendant since, according to this text, Eochaid has no other sons than the three who have revolted, the three who will die in battle. This girl's heroic self-sacrifice, which involves her in a series of carnal, morally questionable relationships, thus has the goal and the effect of saving her father from defeat and from death. We are very close to the heroic self-sacrifice of Yayāti's daughter when she agrees to go from royal bed to royal bed in order to earn those rarest of horses which have been asked of her father and which her father cannot give—this kind of prostitution resulting in the birth of grandsons, who, in their turn, will save their grandfather from another still graver danger.

5. Lugaid Red-Stripes

Behind these correspondences and divergencies, common to the ancestors of Ireland and India and adapted to different circumstances, we perceive the epic illustration of a vast theory of kingship. This theory places in a fundamental opposition the behavior of the king's sons and that of the king's daughters. It contrasts the inevitable political risks inherent in the former with the commercial possibilities offered by marriages of the latter to other kings. It also contrasts the characters of the king's sons with the characters of his grandsons, that is, the sons of his daughters. It justifies a reform, temporary or lasting, in the order of royal succession. And finally, in the person of a princess named after the intoxicating drink **medhu-*, it presents a symbol, and a kind of guarantor or distributor, of the qualities—in accord with the three functions—which kings must synthetically possess.

Such an epic ensemble does not appear elsewhere. At most, in Iran, in the legend to which we alluded in connection with Mādhavī,[53] it was observed that the sons on the one hand, the daughter and her descendants on the other, have contrary destinies: the sons are eliminated, the *xvarrah* (*x*^{v}*arənah*) does not enter into them; instead it enters the daughter, passes into her son and, through him, into the successive representatives of the Kayanid dynasty. But the role attributed to the father here is the inverse of what we find in Yayāti as well as in Eochaid: the father favors his sons, he does what he can to make the *xvarrah* enter them, and when the *xvarrah* has entered his daughter, he persecutes her and desires to kill her. Perhaps this is the result of a Zoroastrian reshaping of the old structure.

Between the Irish and the Indian treatments, the two principal differences—outside the plurality of Eochaid's daughters, perhaps doublets, as opposed to the single daughter of Yayāti—appear to be the following:

1. While Yayāti makes a distribution of the world between his sons dividing it between the good center, purely arya, and the less good or bad sections on the periphery, at least partially barbarian, the episode of Eochaid and his sons has no bearing on the division of Ireland into five Fifths (that of the center, reserved for the supreme king, and the four on the periphery). These Fifths preexist, and the sons, who are only three, or four (the rebellious triplets, and sometimes Conall) are neither in the beginning nor in the course of their lives connected with different territories. The only specification in this sense is the rule concerning the kingship in the center, which the indignant father decrees; but this rule bears (in the *Cath Bóinde*) upon the innocent younger brother, the fourth son, just as much as it does upon the guilty triplets (or their memories).

2. Medb's relation to the three functions is only a moral one, but it is self-conscious and willful and expresses itself in words and acts through her triple claim and the triple demand for qualities (a demand imposed upon her by a *geis*, a "fate" which weighs upon her) which she imposes upon royal candidates. In contrast, it is by carnal creations, in the assortment of grandsons which she gives to her father, by the unconscious mechanism of pregnancies and of what they transmit through heredity, that Mādhavī "expresses" the excellences, distributed among the three functions, which a complete king must normally possess. Another of Eochaid's grandsons, however—the child that another of his daughters, Clothru, has brought forth by her three wicked brothers in order to save her father—may perhaps retain the trace of a more discernible expression of the trifunctional structure. But if this is the case, we must recognize that the content of the three functions is no longer explicit in the texts, which are concerned only with the picturesque, the outer appearance of "Lugaid of the Red Stripes," and not with what these stripes, this bodily tripartition, may at first have signified. He had, says the *Cóir anman*, a circular stripe around the neck, another around the waist. And of the three sections thus marked off, his head resembled that of Nar, his torso that of Bres, and below the belt he was like Lothar.[54] There is certainly nothing functional in the meanings of the fathers' names or in the little that is known about the action of the son, but it should be pointed out that when such real or symbolic divisions of a human or animal body into three (or two, or four) parts are mentioned by some of the Indo-Europeans in their myths, rites, or speculations, they are generally connected with classification or the social expression of the functions. Without going into the political fable of Menenius Agrippa with his "patrician-stomach" and his "plebian-mouth, teeth, limbs, etc.,"[55] the Vedic hymn of the Primordial Man has the four *varṇas* (priests, warriors, tiller-breeders, and *śūdras*) born respectively from the mouth, arms, thighs, and feet of the human victim.[56] In the Indian ritual of the horse sacrifice, three queens perform unctions upon the head, the back, and the rump of the animal about to be immolated, the purpose of which unctions is to assure the royal sacrificer, respectively, or spiritual energy (*tejas*), physical force (*indriya*), and wealth in cattle (*paśu*).[57] Another Indian ritual, that of the *pravargya*, recently

illuminated by J. A. B. van Buitenen,[58] presents a remarkable example of a correspondence between the three segments of the human body (head, trunk, lower body), the three social functions, and the three superimposed parts of the universe. At a certain moment in this ritual, the *adhvaryu* priest pours three oblations of butter while holding the ladle at the level of his face for the first, of his navel for the second, and of his knees for the third. On this occasion he pronounces three formulas, all addressed to a clay figurine called *Gharma*, "warm (milk)," and Mahāvīra, "Great Man." In the first formula, he names heaven and the *brahman* (neuter: principle of the first function and essence of the brahman class); in the second, he names the atmosphere and the *kṣatra* (principle of the second function and essence of the warrior class); and in the third, he names the earth and the *viś* (principle of the third function and essence of the tiller-breeder class). This triple equation certainly bears upon the form of the figurine: three balls of clay joined together, the lower portion flattened out to furnish a base, evoking a man seated in cross-legged position. The three segments marked by the congenital stripes on the body of Lugaid, which are very close to those which the Greek philosophers connected, or, rather, claimed to connect, from top to bottom, with the three functional aspects of the soul—the rational, the passionate, and the concupiscent—may thus initially have indicated that this young man was a perfect synthesis of the qualities which were enunciated a little differently in the triple requirements laid down by his aunt Medb.

The Indian account is in any case of wider scope, and is more harmonious, than the Irish. One may suppose that this latter, cut off from Druidic philosophy like all the epic Irish texts and conserving from the ancient symbols only the interplay of figures and their behavior, has reached us in an impoverished form. But the Indian comparison does afford a glimpse of its primary significance, its value as a structure.[59]

Will it be possible to propose a sociological or psychological interpretation of this structure? Today such an attempt holds only risks. But even now, precautions can be taken against one risk: to judge from the vocabulary of kinship, the oldest Indo-European societies were composed of families defined strictly in relation to the males, to fathers, and sons, and husbands. Accordingly, there is little chance that the conduct of the proud queen Medb, and that of her humble Indian sister Mādhavī, will carry us back to the nebula of matriarchy.[60]

PERSPECTIVES

Our extensive commentary on the fabulous biography of Yayāti is now drawing to a close: he has reascended to heaven with his grandsons and, as far as we know, has never returned. What are we, still on earth, to learn from his legacy?

We have not resolved the "Yima-Yama problem," but we have improved the terms in which to state it and have gathered the elements for new solutions. Either because the material was well conserved from its Indo-Iranian state, or by means of a synthesis peculiar to Iran, Yima is the embodiment of three types, one mythic and two epic, which in India are incarnated in separate figures.

1. By his construction of the subterranean *vara*, in which he has installed—in health and happiness, for an unlimited duration or at least past an anticipated "end of the world"—the chosen specimens of humanity accompanied by specimens of all the animals and all desirable plants, Yima is indeed the homologue of his Indian homonym Yama, king of the blessed realm of the dead. Put simply, this memory of an Indo-Iranian *Yama ruling over a human society of the beyond has been warped and impoverished by the effect of Zoroastrian ideas on the *post mortem* life, by the competition of more strictly Mazdaean conceptions of the "end of the world" and of "paradise," and finally by the substitution of a son of Zoroaster for Yima as the lasting supervisor of the subterranean enclosure, leaving Yima only to build it and to usher in its rightful inhabitants.

2. In his remaining career, consisting of a terrestrial reign, Yima presents traits of which some recall the Indian Vasu Uparicara and

others the Indian Yayāti, two figures who are, in fact, analogous to each other on more than one point.

a. To Vasu Uparicara as to Yima-J̌amšīd belongs the divine favor allowing them to traverse the atmosphere in a crystal chariot; like Yima, Vasu takes this opportunity to establish the grand annual festival of "the opening of time"; like Yima, he loses his privileges as the result of a sin classified as a lie; and again, like Yima, he is involved, on the "losing" side, in disputes over the legitimacy of butchered food.

b. Yayāti, like Yima, is the best example of the type of the "first king" in the sense that Arthur Christensen gave to the term. In different but equivalent ways, they rule over either the progressive peopling or the division and administration of the world; and Yayāti in his own conduct achieves the synthesis, and in the conduct of his grandsons the analysis, of the functions which Yima-J̌amšīd exteriorizes in the creation of the corresponding social classes.

But the most important result of our Indo-Iranian comparisons concerns the sins of these kings, of Yayāti and Vasu Uparicara on the one hand, of Yima on the other.[1] Those of Vasu and of Yima, except in rare aberrant variants, bring on their utter ruin at a single stroke, with neither recourse nor remedy. That of Yayāti is, on the contrary, atoned for, and by a most interesting trifunctional procedure. After an entire life spent amassing merits in the generous use of riches, in the bravery of the conqueror, in the performance of sacrifices, and in the reverence for truth, Yayāti goes to heaven in full beatitude. But there he has a prideful thought which, in a flash, consumes all his merits and sends him hurtling toward earth, toward "hell on earth." But he is saved: his four grandsons transfer upon him the merits which they have acquired, one in the generous use of riches, the second in valor, the third in the performance of sacrifices, and the fourth in truthfulness; they thus reconstitute their grandfather's full stock of merits, and he is able to reascend to heaven. I recalled in this connection the end of the Iranian story of Yima. Long a perfectly virtuous monarch and bearer of the *x^v^arənah*, the visible mark of divine benevolence which assures him of excellence at every level, this king's head is turned one day by an attack of overwhelming pride, a pride which makes him deny God, the ultimate "lie." Immediately the *x^v^arənah* flees him in three fragments, defined according to the three functions, each of which transports itself onto a personage of the future, making one a healer, the second a conqueror, and the third a wise minister. I am not about to take up the comparison again in detail, but I must underline an important point.

Yima sins only once, and yet "three x^v*arənahs*" (*Yašt* 19) or "three portions of x^v*arənah*" (*Dēnkart*) abandon him. What are we to make of this dissymmetry? In 1943 Arthur Christensen sought, by a hypothetical addition to the story, to reestablish the numerical equivalence of causes and effects.

> If the Glory leaves Yima three times or in three portions at three distinct periods, the only conclusion I can draw from this is that Yima, in the Avestan legend, has sinned three times. On the first time, the Glory was acquired by the god of the pact, Miθra, who has connections with the sun. The second time Yima was dethroned and pursued by Dahāka, but the Glory was seized by Θraētaona, who was enabled by it to triumph over Dahāka. Then Yima must have taken possession of the Glory again for a third time and have once again have lost it, after which it was acquired by Kərəsāspa. As I have just said, we find the series Yima-Dahāka-Θraētaona-Kərəsāspa in *Yašts* 5 and 15, where the heroes of antiquity are presented as sacrificing to Anāhitā and to Vayu. Now the hero Θraētaona was not originally considered a king of Iran or of the whole world, but took his place later in the series of first kings. One can thus legitimately suppose that in a more primitive form of the Iranian legend than the one we possess, Yima recovered the crown when Θraētaona overthrew the usurper Dahāka and that he continued his reign until he had committed a new crime.[2]

In 1956, in *Aspects de la fonction guerrière*, I took this idea up.[3] I had just analyzed a legendary schema bound up, in the Indian epic, with Indra, but confirmed as ancient by the Scandinavian Starkaðr-Starcatherus and by the Greek Heracles. I proposed to call it "the three sins of the warrior." In its complete form, it consists of the following: a figure who is a warrior or an eminent champion and, as such, generally useful to the gods or to men, comes nonetheless to commit three successive sins, well separated in time, one in each of the three functional domains (the sacred; warrior morality; riches or sexuality). In certain versions (Indra, Heracles) each sin brings on a punishment, itself linked by its form or by its consequences to the functional domain of the corresponding sin; and, after the third punishment, the guilty party finds that he has undergone a complete despoliation (if he is a god), or is face to face with his own destruction, voluntary or otherwise (if he is human). Understood as Christensen proposed it, the legend of Yima's adversity seemed to me to constitute a parallel: three sins, different from one another in ways we no longer know, but which, according to their consequences, we may suppose to be related to the functions; three losses, themselves plainly functional, those of three thirds of the x^{v}*arənah* relative to religion, agriculture, and martial force, bringing on the complete liquidation of the subject; and finally the appropriation of the thirds of the x^{v}*arənah* by three figures who are themselves characterized functionally (a feature met again in the legend of Indra, where the spiritual energy, force, and beauty lost by the god are absorbed by Dharma, Vāyu, and the two Aśvins, who then make use of them to engender the Pāṇḍavas).

But this comparison had two weak points. First of all, with a unanimity rare in the files on Iranian heroes, from *Yašt* 19 to Ferdowsi and beyond, the texts never attributed more than a single fault to Yima: how can one justify imposing more than this upon him? Moreover, though a complete hero, he is not properly a warrior and it is not as a warrior that he sins but as "universal sovereign." As a result, in the second edition of *Aspects de la fonction guerrière*, recast and completed, which appeared in 1969 under the title *Heur et malheur du guerrier* (translated into English as *Destiny of the Warrior*, 1970),[4] I did not include Yima but left him for the present discussion. If we accept the facts as they present themselves, we touch upon an important distinction.

There is indeed a parallelism between the misfortune of Yima and the misfortunes of Indra in the sense that they are all punishments, they all consist of "losses," and these losses distribute themselves over the three functions. But there is, from the outset, a major difference in the definition of the guilty party.

In brief, in contrast to the "three sins of the warrior," themselves trifunctional, is the single sin, suprafunctional, of the sovereign. Single but irreparable, for it destroys either the raison d'être of sovereignty, namely the protection of the order founded on truth (the sin of lying), or the mystical support of human sovereignties, namely the respect for the superior sovereignty of the gods and the sense of the limitations inherent in every human delegation of that divine sovereignty (the sin of pride). The king falls prey to one or the other of these risks, which, as we have seen, are at bottom reducible to the same thing.

The pathos of this risk is different from that of the risks which result in the "sins of the warrior": in the case of Indra or Heracles we witness the destruction of a being in three phases, by a sort of fatal interlocking, which nonetheless appears to leave a chance, even if not taken or easy to take, for repentance, for rehabilitation. Indeed, up to the last fault, for which he accepts the punishment with dignity, Heracles' life is passed in self-purification, expiation. The "single sin of the king," lying or pride, or lying-pride, calls for something quite different: the blow, administered without delay and with no possibility of redress, which destroys all the roots and fruits of a most excellent good fortune. One is reminded of the Judeo-Christian Satan, or the Iblis of the Quran, who had first been the most noble creature, the most richly favored, and even the most faithful.

This contrasting of the single sin of the sovereign with the three sins of the warrior also conforms to the different natures of the two human types and to their different relations to the structure of the three functions. The sovereign comprises within himself the very synthesis of the principles of these functions, so that a single sin by him, one which is proper to him and always—lying, impiety, tyranny—a form of pride, affects all three functional zones at one blow; whereas the warrior, placed by definition at a single level of the trifunctional structure, loses himself completely only if he perseveres in his wickedness, if he commits in succession a sin against the principles of each of the functions, that is to say, three sins. It should not be assumed, then, as Arthur Christensen did, that in an older form of the legend, Yima had sinned three times.

The speculations that are beginning to emerge here must be very old. The Celts present nothing of this sort, it seems, but other Western Indo-Europeans do provide some testimony. If one accepts the interpretation which I proposed thirty years ago for the legends about the four pre-Etruscan kings of Rome,[5] the first book of Livy furnishes a variant—one which can scarcely be fortuitous—of this very theme. In the main, the demigod-founder Romulus and the jurist-priest Numa give Rome the advantages of the first function—*auspicia, sacra, leges;* Tullus Hostilius, the purely warrior king, gives her the advantages of the second, *arma* and military science; and the third function, based upon wealth and economic development, takes form next under Ancus Marcius. Now, of these four kings, two meet catastrophic ends because they have sinned—Romulus and Tullus. But the sins and the catastrophes are very different. In the case of Romulus, whose power intoxicates him and who becomes, late in life, an insufferable tyrant whom the senators are at least suspected of having made suddenly disappear—in expectation of his becoming a god[6]—there is but one sin and one penalty. In the case of Tullus, there are two sins, one of the first and one of the second function, and two punishments of increasing importance, for it is he who scorns religion and neglects the cult of the gods, who then refuses all rest to his soldiers, not even sparing them during an epidemic, and whom the gods punish first by afflicting his body with the same sickness that exhausts his soldiers, and then by casting his thoughts into such a clumsy caricature of religion that he draws the thunderbolt down upon himself in the course of a badly made invocation.[7] If the sin of the third function—concerning sex—is missing from the tableau of this warrior king, it is probably because the Roman tradition reserved it for the last king, who was also bellicose, and whose fall it provoked: this is the etiological myth of the *regifugium*, the violation of Lucretia by Sextus Tarquinius, son of the Excessive.[8] It seems then that we might have, in a diptych constructed as carefully as everything else in the "history" of Rome's origins, a contrasting use of the two themes.

To return to the multiple Indian correspondance with Yima, I can at this point, short of a demonstration which is beyond the scope of this book, only repeat my preference: everything can be more easily understood if the Iranian Yima drew upon himself three types that were distinct in Indo-Iranian times and have remained so throughout Indian tradition. An important argument in this direction is the following. In India, the three royal types are connected with ritual actions that are all clearly different: Yama intervenes only in the funerary ritual in which the newly dead are made over to him; Vasu Uparicara founds the annual royal festival of Indra's Garland;

and the adventure of Yayāti and his grandsons unfolds during a *vājapeya*, a ceremony that is royal, political, and not periodical—and this is certainly not a chance selection, since the two principal rites of the *vājapeya* are a symbolic ascent to heaven and a chariot race which the king is supposed to win,[9] two features in full correspondence with the story of Yayāti, which closes with a chariot race along the way that ascends to heaven.

The antiquity of two of these rituals is not in doubt. Yima's *vara*, distorted as it is, suffices to establish as Indo-Iranian the conception of Yama as king of the beyond. And the circumstances of the foundation of the festival of Indra's Garland (the king's voyage through the air in a crystal chariot) too nearly recall those of the Iranian Nawrōz for there not to be a common tradition behind them both. As to the rites of the *vājapeya*, I plan in a later work to show that they go still farther back. In these conditions, it is easier to think that the Iranian Yima, dispossessed by the Zoroastrian reform of his function as king of the beyond, has reunited upon himself legends that were primitively bound up with two distinct rituals of earthly kingship.

The Indo-Iranian problem, which was our starting point, has opened out, on the other hand, on a larger Indo-European scale. With the exception—a natural one given the difference of the Celtic and Indo-Iranian pieties—of the scenes involving the king's sins and their consequences, we have seen the entire structure of the biography of the universal king Yayāti overlap that of the biography of Eochaid Feidlech, the supreme king of Ireland. We have here two good, indeed excellent kings (Yayāti's sin, a fugitive prideful thought, seems to us a small matter indeed). Eochaid had the best of reputations, and the Irish of the middle ages, fond of etymologies whether true or false, explained his surname Feidlech as a derivative of *feidel*, "just," because, says the *Cath Bóinde*, he was "just toward all." Likewise, Yayāti has remained in Indian thought the very model for good kings: in a lengthy description of the sort of golden age enjoyed, after the birth of the Buddha-to-be, by his father's kingdom, the poet of the *Buddhacarita* compares the state of virtue which flourished then to the reign of only one former king: Yayāti, son of Nahuṣa (2,11). The domestic sorrows which afflict both kings and which affect them deeply do not result from any fault of their own:

they are subjected to them. And in connection with these two figures of the same rank, of the same character, Ireland and India have depicted, in a dramatic fashion, two similarly styled sets of relationships—with their rebellious sons on the one hand, and with their respectful and devoted daughters on the other. From this general accord a still more precise correspondence, thoroughly "improbable" in the sense which mathematicians give to the word, can be seen between the two feminine figures with nearly identical names: Medb, principal daughter of Eochaid, and Mādhavī, sole daughter of Yayāti. Both being wives of multiple kings, they themselves guarantee, or are entrusted with, the virtues a king must possess on the three functional levels. Certainly we have here, conserved on the one side by the Druids, on the other in the unwritten "fifth Veda" from which the post-Vedic narratives of India in large part derive, a fragment of Indo-European politico-religious philosophy, that is, some of the speculations made by the Indo-Europeans on the status and the destiny of kings. Significantly, we are really dealing on both sides with human epic, built upon a religious foundation, of course, and with many marvels, but one in which the gods (even those in the Indian account) do not play the leading role. Comparative study thus allows us to work back not to a theological or mythological schema but to an Indo-European literary theme.

And naturally, a literary work does not have to set forth a theory: it is the hearer's or the reader's task to perceive the providential design which has arranged the events in the order in which the work presents them and with the results it describes. Yet it is the design that justifies these events and results, and gives them a meaning.

To limit ourselves to the episode of Mādhavī: when Yayāti delivers his daughter over to the brahman who demands alms from him that he is unable to give, he cannot foresee that this gift will result in the birth of four grandsons who will later rehabilitate him; when Mādhavī proposes to bear four sons to four kings, she cannot foresee that each will excel as a king in one function and that they will consequently be fit, when united, to reconstitute the treasure of royal merits which their grandfather will need; and then, when she refuses to marry for good and retires into the forest, she cannot foresee that she will accumulate merits which her father will need as well; when the four grandsons themselves join together to celebrate a *vājapeya*, they cannot foresee that their grandfather will fall amongst them, that they will have the occasion to transfer their merits upon him, and that this heroic act will make them worthy of accompanying him on his reascension to heaven. But all this is known to the gods or, what amounts to the same thing, to the author of the saga; and we too, progressively, come to recognize a unity and a finality beneath the variety and apparent whims of chance.

As is typical in accounts from medieval Ireland, which no longer rely upon a religion or even upon a living ideology, the story of Eochaid, of his daughters Medb and Clothru and his grandson Lugaid, is still more laicized and worked over as literature—despite the marvels which are still found in it. But the "lessons," as we have seen, are the same. In a fashion different from Mādhavī, but, like her, passing from husband to husband, Medb guarantees the permanence or the renewal of the triad of royal virtues defined according to the three functions. If she does not, like Mādhavī, do it for her father's benefit, it is because the Irish authors have divided the task between her and the foremost of her sisters: Medb provides for the establishment of "good" kingdoms, whoever their head may be; and it is Clothru who saves her royal father by sacrificing herself, by delivering herself over to an incestuous triple embrace from which will be born a tripartite (and probably originally trifunctional) son, the immediate object of which, however, is to weaken her father's adversaries and to deprive them of the victory which, without this intervention, they would certainly have won. All of this is less simple, less linear than the chain of events in the Indian story. The Irish account, on the other hand, makes for a stronger connection than does the Indian between the two episodes which form the king's biography. In Yayāti's case, there is no more than a succession, with neither logical links nor imbrication, between the disrespect or the rebellion of his sons, the devotion of his daughter, and the service of his grandsons. Mādhavī saves her father, not from his sons' disrespect or rebellion, but from a fall brought on later by a grave sin which he himself commits. On the contrary, it is to save her father from her brothers that Clothru heroically decides upon the triple incest. And she does save him—all by herself, since the tripartite son whom she bears on this occasion does not appear to have played a part in aiding his grandfather other than by his conception, by the debilitation which the act of procreation produces among his three fathers.

But another more important difference takes us beyond the literature. It has been noted briefly above, but it must be taken up again here, for it opens up a new perspective on the operation of Indo-European kingship. In neither of their lives and in none of their services are Medb or Clothru under any obligation to remain virgins or to conduct themselves as virgins. On the contrary: Medb places princes on the throne by marrying them, and her sister Clothru, before or after her triple sacrifice—which apparently troubles her as an act of incest but not as a sexual union—is included among the daughters that Eochaid gives to Conchobar. Mādhavī, on the other hand, is fundamentally a virgin.

To be sure, many are the young women, in the *Mahābhārata* and generally in Indian traditions, who have in one way or another received the privilege of recovering their virginity, either immediately after having graciously given it to a god or a saint, or after the birth of the infant that this embrace has produced. We are reminded of Kuntī, the mother of the three eldest Pāṇḍavas, of their great grandmother Satyavatī, and also of Draupadī, the Pāṇḍavas' common wife. Indeed the latter, whom the five brothers possess successively, cyclically, according to a usage of the time agreed upon in advance, even recovers her virginity each time she changes husbands. In their diversity, however, all these women have one trait in common: their later life is that of an ordinary woman, namely that of a wife and mother. Once it is recovered, none remains or wishes to remain in possession of her virginity for future occasions: they all marry and, in general, hide from their husbands the adventure of their youth. The peculiarity of Yayāti's daughter is that she chooses to remain a virgin, if one may put it this way, as soon as she can—as soon as she has accomplished, in four temporary unions, the task assigned her by the brahman who had received her as a gift from her father. Once free, she refuses the marriage which would have been her true marriage, goes to live in the forest—virgin forever—and concerns herself no more with her sons. Even for the procreation of these sons, she conducts herself neither as a wife nor as a mother: she is only a consenting but uninvolved instrument, shrewd and unfeeling, untouched by the quadruple event, morally as well as physically. Out of obedience she simply accepts, and even directs, the four-year suspension of her virginal vocation. Now these are the two phases of her life which, through their combined effects, finally save and restore her father: the functional merits of the sons that she has borne in exceptional circumstances, plus the reinforcement of half of the undifferentiated merits which she herself has won by her ascetic forest life, compensate for Yayāti's fault and, when transferred onto him, regain him his place among the royal saints. The fact that the action occurs partly in heaven, partly on earth, at first during the protagonist's life and then after his death, changes nothing essential: we are in India, where the two worlds adjust to each other and interpenetrate.

To be sure, the merits which Mādhavī wins in the forest and later transmits to her father are those which are won uniformly by men and women who, at whatever moment of their lives, choose the forest: it is not in her capacity as a virgin, not through the jealous cultivation of her virginity, that she acquires her efficacy, but through depriving herself of food, comfort, etc., in short, through a kind of dehumanization. But it is still as a virgin that she chooses the forest: not at the end of a routine existence, having become sterile, or to attend a discontented or aged husband, but in full youth, on the day provided for her marriage, during the ceremony, before an assembly of the most prestigious suitors. That is what gives her decision its particular coloring, making of her, as much as it could in pre-Buddhist India, the counterpart of the young princesses of the West who shunned the most glittering matches in favor of the cloth, prayer, and the divine Bridegroom.

In brief, in the providential plan which guides her without her knowing it, but which reveals itself little by little to the reader and perhaps to her as well, she has a unique and continuous role: to prepare for the king's salvation. And it is a role that she fills through her virginal nature, indeed her vocation as a virgin, which permits her first to give birth, without becoming a true wife, to the four masculine saviors of her father the king, and then impels her into the forest, where, still unconsciously, she puts herself in a position to intervene as his fifth and decisive savior. Thus, in a narrative, novel-like form, reworked into more recent conceptions, we catch sight of one element of an ancient ideology of the royal function: we understand how virginity—conserved physically and, to an even greater extent, morally by a woman close to the king, in this case by his closest relative—was important and efficacious in protecting the king against the risks of his position.

Let us now cross to the other extremity of the Indo-European world, to the Italic peoples, the Romans, whose religious vocabulary presents such remarkable concordances with the Indian—one of these being the very name for a king, *rēg-*.[10] From Rome too, or rather from Alba, we could draw upon a legend, a beautiful romance, that of the youthful exploits of the founding king. Numitor, Romulus' grandfather, has also lost the kingship, not because he has sinned, but —another risk of the royal function—through a dispossession brought on through his own naïve honesty; and he too is finally restored by his daughter's son, a son born in an exceptional and marvelous way from a daughter who is a virgin, indeed, *virgo Vestalis*, *ἄγαμος καί παρθένος*, as specified by Plutarch (*Romulus*, 3,4). Here there is only one grandson, but he is by himself as complete, as trifunctional, as the grandsons of Yayāti combined. This is demonstrated by his entire reign and, theologically, by his successive connections with the three gods of the precapitoline triad: Mars is his father, Jupiter is his unique and constant protector, and he himself, after his death, becomes Quirinus. But Rome furnishes something better than a legend: a clear ritual structure.

We know only the *rex* of republican times, reduced to a purely sacerdotal role. But the religious conservatism of the Romans is such that whatever concerns the *rex* is from a past that has hardened and fossilized in its prerepublican form. In particular there is the *regia*, the *regia domus*, on the Forum. In the historic period, the *rex* and the *regina* do not live there: the *regia* is essentially the department of the grand pontiff, who has taken onto himself the most active part of the religious heritage of the king. But it still remains, in name, the "house of the king," and rituals like that of the October Horse, on the Ides of the first month of autumn, make sense only if the *regia*, which holds an important place in them, is understood in this fashion.

Now this king's house, as I pointed out some time ago,[11] seems to constitute in the very plan of its construction the topographic synthesis of the three functions, those which the *rex*, in royal times, had to make into an active synthesis. For not only is Romulus, the first king of legend, trifunctional, directly attached at once to Jupiter, Mars, and Quirinus, but every holder of the *regnum* must be so as well.[12] This is what justifies his juxtaposition to the three *flamines maiores*, who are themselves rigorously specialized. The flamen of Jupiter, that of Mars, and that of Quirinus each maintain passively and separately and for the benefit of Rome (and, before the Republic, for the benefit of the *rex*), a narrow and permanent contact with the cosmic "function" covered by the name of the corresponding god: magico- and juridico-religious sovereignty for the *Dialis;* martial force for the *Martialis;* and organized abundance—a peaceful abundance of men and of the means of sustenance—for the *Quirinalis*. The *rex* is at the "controls" of the chariot of state; and in this position he uses, as need arises, one or the other of these contacts—assured him by the *flamines*—with the three forces necessary for the life of society and of the world. He must thus possess their synthesis, not in himself but in front of him, at his disposal. And this is just what is expressed by the plan of the *regia* as it was built in the valley of the Forum in the fifth century, certainly reproducing in its singularity a traditional symbolic layout—probably the form of the first *regia* of the Palatine, anterior to the extension of the city. The main body of the building, in front of the court, has the form of a very elongated trapezoid, almost rectangular, divided into three consecutive rooms—one large, containing a hearth, and two contiguous smaller ones—the central one, to judge from the symmetric traces of sills on the long sides of the trapezoid, appearing to have been a passageway between the exterior and the courtyard. The uses of each of the rooms may be discussed, but their number corresponds to what we know from the texts. The *regia* was, for the most part, open; it served for acts of public administration and public cult that were carried out by the persons one would expect, the *rex*, the *regina*, and the *flaminica dialis*. But it also contained two *sacraria*, chapels, that were, on the contrary, closed, secret, accessible only to special persons and in precise circumstances: a *sacrarium Martis* and a *sacrarium Opis Consivae.*

In the first were conserved the *hastae Martis,* whose spontaneous trembling was a menacing omen. Mars could have no temple in the interior of the *pomerium,* and this chapel was not a temple. It merely sheltered, in the king's house, powerful symbols of Mars's mode of action. Its presence expressed that the *rex,* in addition to his constant exercise of the politico-religious administration of the first function, had at his disposal the essence and the means of the second function.

A similar possession is expressed, for the third function, by the presence of the carefully closed chapel of Ops, Abundance personified—especially Abundance resulting from the harvest—under the name Ops *Consiva,* which surely signifies the Abundance that is not yet utilized, that is stored (*condita*), kept in reserve.[13]

Which personages are said to be authorized to go inside these two chapels? First, negatively, let us observe that none of the three *flamines maiores*—who, as we have just recalled, are the respective guarantors of permanent mystical contact between Rome and Jupiter, between Rome and Mars, and between Rome and Quirinus—is so authorized. No text shows any of them in the *regia.* At the first level it is not the *flamen Dialis* but his wife, the *flaminica,* who comes there to sacrifice a ram to Jupiter on all *nundinae*—market days, formerly days of political activity, of contact between the king and the people (Macrobius, *Saturnalia,* I,16,30). The *flamen Martialis* is not recorded in the *sacrarium Martis.* And the very words of Varro which tell us about the chapel of Ops Consiva debar the *flamen Quirinalis* from entering it. This latter exclusion is all the more remarkable as it is he who assures the cult of Consus, the god theologically paired with Ops Consiva (Tertullian, *De spectaculis,* 5). It is known that Ops is honored twice during the year, in the summer on August 25th, and on the eve of winter on December 19th, and that on each occasion her festival is preceded, three days earlier, by one for Consus, on August 20th and December 15th. This interval is enough to attest to a liaison between the two festivals and the two divinities: on the one hand, the god of the gathering of crops, of storage, and on the other, the goddess of stored-up abundance. Now on August 21st, at the subterranean altar of Consus on the Field of Mars, the *flamen Quirinalis* and the Vestal virgins officiate together, whereas, after the interval of three days in the chapel of Ops *in regia*, one can deduce from the text of Varro (*De lingua latina*, 6,21) that the Vestal virgins officiate alone.

Thus the major flamens seem to be strangers to the administration of the three functions as practiced in the *regia*. Even the first, the Dialis, merely delegates his wife for the periodic sacrifices performed there, and she, to tell the truth, is nearly as sacred as he is. But then, who does get into the two secret chapels of Mars and Ops?

As to the chapel of Ops, the passage from Varro to which I just referred says: "There was in the *regia* a chapel of Ops Consiva that was so holy that none but the *virgines Vestales* and the *sacerdos publicus* could enter it"—that is to say, on the one hand the vestal virgins, on the other the "priest of the state," the Grand Pontiff. The latter's right of entry was probably justified by the fact that in the republican period, he was the master of the house, the occupant of the *regia* in place of the *rex*. As to the Vestal virgins, it is natural to think that their visit to this chapel, or at least one of their visits, took place on the day of the festival of the goddess who resided there, on the Opeconsivia of August 25th; and they probably came for a sacrifice, since Festus (p. 354 L^2) speaks of a vase of a particular type which was peculiar to sacrifices offered *in sacrario Opis Consivae*.

Of the chapel of Mars we know two things. Servius (*Ad Aen.*, 8,3; 7,603) says that, once war was declared, and before going to take his command, the general-in-chief designate entered the *sacrarium Martis* and shook the bucklers, then the lance of the god's *simulacrum*, saying "*Mars vigila!*" This general *imperaturus* himself, like the Grand Pontiff in other matters, is also an heir of the prehistoric *rex*, who in all legends without exception, from Romulus down to the second Tarquin, was sole commander of the armies. His visit to the "Mars of the king" is thus natural. But we also know through Festus (p. 419 L^2) that a sacrifice (not specified) was offered *in regia* by the *Saliae virgines*, the "Salian virgins," clothed like the Salian warrior-priests, *Salii, cum apicibus paludatae*. It is more than probable, since the *Salii* are the priests of Mars, that the *virgines Saliae* who sacrificed in the *regia* did so in the part of the *regia* reserved for Mars.

Thus, aside from the *imperator* in one case and the *sacerdos publicus* in the other, both of them republican replacements for the king in matters concerning the conduct of war and the control of religion, the cults of the second and third function are maintained, in the royal house, by *virgines*: Salian virgins, Vestal virgins. Why? The lessons of the Indian legend of Yayāti can help us to understand.

To be a virgin, to remain a virgin, is not simply to be chaste. Chastity is of the order of purity; virginity is something higher, of the order of plenitude. A woman who remains a virgin conserves in herself, unutilized but not destroyed, intact and as if reinforced by her will, the creative power that is hers by nature. In religious usage, the virgin woman is apt, at her high point, to symbolize and thus to assure the function of holding in reserve, and conserving "for all useful purposes," the various powers needed by society and, primarily, by the head of society, the king. In this way, there is an exact correspondence between what the virgin priestesses represent in the sacerdotal community and what is represented materially by the *sacrarium Martis* and the *sacrarium Opis Consivae* in the house of the king: warrior force held in reserve, and stored-up Abundance. In the Indian legend it was not through a cult or in chapels that Yayāti's virgin daughter assured her father of a "reserve store" of the advantages of the diverse functions. She did this, rather, through her flesh, through the sons that she formed within herself and gave birth to in an exceptional manner, each a specialist in one of the functions, without actually ceasing to be a virgin. And second, she did it through the merits which she herself acquired and accumulated in her final career as a virgin turned ascetic. On the day when the king needed these reserves, having succumbed to one of the risks inherent in the royal function, they were ready for him: those who held them, the girl and her four sons, had only to transmit them. But Rome's ritual structure and India's legendary structure present the same teaching, the latter with such imaginative liberties as a "virgin mother" and "virgin's sons" which a ritual like the Roman one, constrained to respect the laws of nature, could not have permitted.

There is, however, a notable difference between the Indian legend and the Roman ritual. All the functions are presented differentially in Yayāti's daughter and her sons—including the first function, which is represented by two particularly important qualities: faultless veracity and the assiduous practice of sacrifices. On the contrary, in the *regia* there is no homogeneity between the first function and the other two, neither in the dimensions and distribution of the premises nor in the officiating personnel. Mars and Ops are lodged only in the *regia*, in special chapels, while the activities of the first function, most notably certain sacrifices received by the high gods, are performed in the whole group of buildings. As far as we know, there are three such sacrifices: those received by (1) Jupiter on all *nundinae*, (2) Juno on all calends, and (3) Janus at the beginning of each year. Apparently virgins take care of the cult only in the two chapels, for Mars and for Ops. When it comes to the cults of the "sovereign" divinities, those of the first function—apart from the *rex* himself, who sacrifices to Janus on January 9th (Ovid, *Fastes*, I,318; Varro, *De lingua latina*, 3,12)—they are still performed exclusively by women. But now they are married priestesses, priestesses for whom marriage is a condition and an important element in their sacerdotal status: it is the *flaminica Dialis* (I stress that it is she and not her husband) who sacrifices every nine days to Jupiter (Macrobius, I,16,30), and it is the *regina sacrorum* who sacrifices to Juno on the first day of each month (Macrobius, I,15,18). A remarkable structure thus emerges here: (1) the only males operating in the *regia* are the *rex* and his republican representatives (*imperator; sacerdos publicus*); (2) outside of them, the religious activities of the *regia* are carried out by women; (3) these activities are performed by married priestesses, those of highest rank, for the divinities of the first function; and (4) they are performed by two types of virgin priestesses for the divinities of the second and third functions.

What is signified here is that at the level of the first function, that of Jupiter the celestial *rex*, and also, essentially, at the level of the terrestrial *rex* (from which come his special connections, among the three major flamens, with the flamen of Jupiter), nothing is held in reserve: the religious life, or the politico-religious life, is here an actuality, a continuous *do ut des*. On the contrary, for war, which is fortunately not permanent and which was at first seasonal, and for the storage of Abundance, which is by nature seasonal, the placing on reserve of the powers of Mars and Ops is the sole means of seeing to it that they are continually maintained at the king's disposal.

Perhaps this identity of status should be related to a similar parallelism, of a formulistic kind, between the rituals of the two *sacraria*. When the general-in-chief comes to touch the lances of Mars before taking his command, he says: *Mars, vigila!* And we know (also from Servius, ibid., 10,228) that once a year the Vestal virgins accost the king by saying: *Vigilasne rex? Vigila!* Servius does not specify the circumstance in which this step is taken, but we are not without means of interpretation. The gloss is attached to a verse of the *Aeneid* and indicates that it is a ritual expression, scarcely modified, which Vergil has employed in this passage. Now in Vergil the circumstances are clear: it is a sequel to the episode in which the Trojan ships are burned and changed into nymphs. While Aeneas has embarked to seek reinforcements, Turnus and the Latins manage to set fire to the fleet which Aeneas left at anchor before his camp, near the mouths of the Tiber. But Cybele immediately metamorphoses the hulls into nymphs, and the foremost of these nymphs swims to meet Aeneas and, catching him at his ship, says to him: *Vigilasne, deum gens Aenea? Vigila!* Now it is easy to see that, in this episode of the burning of the ships, Vergil wanted to bring together the equivalents of the various divinities to whom a cult is rendered at the Volcanalia, Vulcan's festival against fires—notably, given the season, harvest fires and grain fires.[14] The divinities thus represented are Vulcan, obviously in his capacity as the destroying fire, Ops, the nymphs with—we can assume—Juturna at their head, and Quirinus. Now, in the episode of the *Aeneid*, "Ops" is translated into Greek by "Cybele" (as was commonly done even in Vergil's day);[15] the principal nymph receives another name (Cymodocea)—Juturna being the patroness of terrestrial fountains and, moreover, for Vergil, the enemy of the Trojans; and Quirinus, impossible since for Vergil he is no more than a deified Romulus, is replaced by Aeneas himself, the customary prefiguration of Romulus in the poem.[16] Now the Volcanalia rites are celebrated on August 23d, that is, in the middle of the three days intercalated between the Consualia of the 21st and the Opiconsivia of the 25th, and it is certain that they form a structured group with these two rites. Thus if Vergil imparts to the nymph, in the sequel of a scene inspired by the Volcanalia, the words of appeal which the Vestals address to the *rex* in an unspecified ritual circumstance, it is likely that we are dealing with an appeal that was made following the Volcanalia, that is, either at the

Opiconsivia rites themselves, or just before them. What is of interest is that the appeal of the imperator in the *sacrarium Martis* and the appeal of the Vestals to the *rex* in the cultic zone of Ops Consiva employ the same word: *vigila*. Against the enemy that Rome is about to face, and also to counteract the fire that threatens stored-up abundance, what is demanded in the *regia* at the levels of the second and third functions is "vigilance," whether on the part of the god Mars or on the part of the king. The vigilance which precedes action, which waits and keeps watch but does not manifest itself, is the very attitude which accords with the sort of mystical benefits that the two chapels of the *regia* are supposed to contain: advantages, opportunities, means held in reserve until they are used, and ready to be used.

It will be profitable to examine the other Indo-European societies whose royal mechanisms are more or less well known. If Ireland, with Medb and Clothru, entrusts the royal function or the salvation of the king—*rí* or *ardrí*—to women who are in no way virgins, the best known among the Celts of Great Britain, the Welsh, adhere to the Roman model in a brief, single, but important piece of legend. At the beginning of the fourth branch of the *Mabinogi*, it is said that the magician-king Math, except in times of war, always had to keep his feet in the lap of a virgin girl.[17] The reflections we have just made on the relations between virgins and the *rex* explain this strange condition, at least in principle if not in form.

As to the Scandinavians, they conform at once to both the Roman and the Indian models: as in Rome, the male and female sovereigns have virgin auxiliaries, but, as in India, the first function is, from this standpoint, homogeneous with the other two. Moreover, the testimony comes neither from a ritual like Rome's nor from a saga like India's, but from theology and myth.

The highest level of the Scandinavian pantheon is occupied by a royal couple, Óðinn and Frigg. The wife's conduct, at least, is without weakness, worthy of the Roman matrons: she is a serious spouse and a good mother. Óðinn and Frigg also provide the model for the human household, which is constituted with their permission. There exists a special minor goddess, a personified abstraction named Lofn, whose service Snorri (*Gylfaginning*, 36)[18] defines as follows: "She is so gentle and so good to those who invoke her, men and women, that she obtains for them, from All-father (= Óðinn) and Frigg, permission to contract marriages, even when their union was first forbidden or banned." Such is the couple, with the spouse of the king of the gods, like the Roman *regina*, participating modestly but actively in the sovereign function of her husband. What do we know of Óðinn and Frigg's collaborators?

At the third level they have at their disposal the goddess Fulla—a synonym of the Roman Ops, Abundance personified. Fulla is not a Vanir goddess, as one might expect, but rather one of the Æsir. She is attached specifically to the person of Frigg. Snorri (*Gylfaginning*, 22)[19] defines her thus: "She wears her hair loose (*laushár*), with a golden band (*gullband*) around her head. She carries Frigg's little box (*eski Friggjar*), looks after her shoes (*gætir skóklæda hennar*), and knows her secret decisions (*launrad*)." Her close connection with the sovereign couple is confirmed by a feature of the myth of Baldr: from the bottom of the underworld, from the kingdom of Hel, Baldr and his wife send presents to only three Æsir: the magic ring Draupnir to Óðinn, a pretty blouse and other unspecified objects to Frigg, and a gold ring to Fulla (*Gylfaginning*, 34 end).[20] Virgins are not numerous among the Æsir: this goddess, Abundance at the service of the royal couple, is a virgin: *hon er mær*.

At the second level, that of the warrior, through an evolution proper to the Germans, Óðinn is more involved than are the sovereign gods of India and even of Rome: witness his connections with combatants, in battle itself and, beyond, in Valhöll where he welcomes the heroic dead. Now his auxiliaries in this function are not masculine figures but the *Valkyrjur*, who see that the perpetual banquets of Valhöll are properly provided for and even recruit the guests who attend them. "Óðinn," says Snorri (*Gylfaginning*, 22 end[21]), sends them to every battle, and they choose those of the men who will fall (*þær kjósa feigð á menn*), and award victory (*ráða sigri*)." Now the Valkyries, barring a romantic accident, are and remain virgins. In an account by Saxo Grammaticus,[22] they introduce themselves to a hero by saying that "the lot of wars, *fortuna bellorum*, is above all regulated by their intervention, *suis ductibus auspiciisque*, that they often take part in combats, *praeliis interesse*, without letting anyone see them, and, through clandestine assistance, assure success for their friends." But the word by which the historian introduces them is no less important in describing them: *virgines.*

As to the first level, that of sovereignty properly speaking, to whom does Óðinn, a euhemerized Óðinn, owe the possession, the very existence, of his first Scandinavian kingdom—a Danish stopping-place in his march toward the Swedish Upland? To a goddess, Gefjun. And here is the sentence that Snorri devotes to her in his enumeration of the female Æsir, just before speaking of Fulla (*Gylfaginning*, 22):[23] "Gefjun is a virgin (*hon er mær*), and those who die virgins serve her in the other world" (*ok henni þjóna þær, er meyjar andaz*). Such is the theological definition, but there is also a legend about her that has been historicized (*Ynglingasaga*, 5; cf. *Gylfaginning*, 1). Arriving at the shore of Baltic Straits, Óðinn, the "king," sends Gefjun further to the north, toward the Swedish king Gylfi, to ask him for lands. The Swede—in a variant of a well-known theme[24]—grants her whatever she can plow in a day and a night. She thus goes to the land of the giants and there, though a virgin and protector of virgins, she makes herself produce four sons by a giant, transforms them into oxen, and yokes them to a plow. They draw so energetically that they are able to detach a large piece from Gylfi's kingdom. And this piece, hurled toward the south beyond the coast, becomes the Danish island of Zealand, Óðinn's first kingdom, in which, however, he will not remain since it is his calling to rule in Sweden itself in place of Gylfi. Thus Gefjun has rendered her master the most urgent service a king could need: she has procured for him, in material terms, a kingdom.[25] Naturally the exegetes are embarrassed by this contradiction: as a goddess, Gefjun is a virgin and protector of virgins; in "history," she makes herself produce four sons by a giant to give a kingdom to the king.[26] But the same aporia is enacted in the legend of Mādhavī: a virgin by vocation and destined to spend the remainder of her life in virginity, she first commits herself, out of obedience, to the production of four sons who, with her, on the day of his need, will restore her royal father, and who, with her, in the matter of immediate moment, will save him from the shame of a refusal to give alms.

These interconnections are not banal. They compel us to admit that the Indo-Europeans had already constructed a well-articulated theory about the irreplaceable services which virgin collaborators, lastingly virgin, living reserves of power and efficacy, rendered to their kings, whether on all three functional levels, or only, as in Rome, on the second and third.

The suppression, or even the overturning, of the virginal condition in the Irish legend, which is in other respects so close to that of Yayāti and Mādhavī, poses a problem I must leave to the Celticists: on this point Ireland confronts a remarkable coalition of India, Rome, Scandinavia, and Wales.

NOTES

Introduction

1. To avoid confusion, I use the form Yima for the Iranian figure, reserving Yama for the Indian.

2. What follows is reprinted from the second essay of *Rituels indo-européens à Rome*, 1954, "Aedes rotunda Vestae"; I wish to thank the Éditions Klincksieck for permitting its reappearance.

3. Provisionally, see *Les dieux des Indo-Européens* (1952), chapter 2, "Les dieux souverains," with substantial changes in the Spanish edition, *Los Dioses de los Indoeuropeos* (1970), pp. 39–68; and *Mythe et épopée* I (1968), pp. 147–51.

4. William Dwight Whitney, trans., *Atharva-Veda Samhitā* (repr., 1962), slightly modified; the following *AV* verses also from Whitney's translation.

5. Most recently, with a rich bibliography, Peter Snoy, *Die Kafiren: Formen der Wirtschaft und geistiger Kultur* (Inaugural dissertation, Frankfort a.M., 1962), pp. 126–35.

6. Stig Wikander, "Vedique *kshaita*, avestique *xšaēta*," *Studia Linguistica* 5 (1951): 89–94.

7. Arthur Christensen, *Les types du premier homme et du premier roi dans l'histoire légendaire des Iraniens*, II: *Yim* (1934), p. 45: "Among the Iranians, Yima is never elevated to the sphere of the gods. But the legend of Yima is developed in two directions and forms itself into two legends of Yima which exist side by side, even though the one would logically have to exclude the other: on the one hand there is Yima the first man and first sovereign of the earth; later, when he is displaced by Gayōmart, Hōšang, and Taxmōruw, he keeps his role as one of the first kings of the earth; on the other hand, the popular tradition—and the imagination of the priests—places Yima, as the central figure, in the nonterrestrial land of the blessed. The thread which tied together the two phases of the first man's existence is broken."

8. Cf. *Zand-Ākāsīh, Iranian or Greater Bundahišn* 32,6 and 10, ed. B. T. Anklesaria (Bombay, 1956), p. 270.

9. Christensen, pp. 16–18; cf. Herman Lommel, *Die Yäšts des Awesta* (1927), appendix, pp. 196–207.

10. From Christensen's French translation.

11. Georges Dumézil, "La préhistoire indo-iranienne des castes," *Journal Asiatique* 216 (1930): 113–14; Émile Benveniste, "Les classes sociales dans la tradition avestique," ibid. 221 (1932): 119.

12. On a possible correspondence that is more precise, see Dumézil "La, *sabhā* de Yama," *Journal Asiatique* 253 (1965): 161–65.

13. Concerning incest on the level of the third function, see my *From Myth to Fiction*, trans. Derek Coltman (Chicago, 1973), chapter 4, "Hadingus with Harthgrepa: legitimate incest among the Vanes".

14. See *Mythe et épopée* II (1971), part 2, "Entre les dieux et les démons: un sorcier," on Kāvya Uśanas and Kavi Usan, especially pp. 158–59, 229–38.

Chapter 1

1. Five times *páñca kṣitáyaḥ*; three times *p. carṣaṇáyaḥ*; five times *p. kr̥ṣṭáyaḥ*; eleven times *p. janā́saḥ*; to which Schlerath adds with good reason the adjective *pā́ncajanaya* (seven times) and the elliptical expressions *p. mā́nuṣāḥ* (once) and *p. priyā́ḥ* (once).

2. *Das Königtum im Rig- und Atharvaveda* (1960), pp. 28–32. The references and the early bibliography are cited there, as well as in the posthumous article of D. B. Kosambi, "The Vedic 'Five Tribes,'" *Journal of the American Oriental Society* 87 (1967): 33–39 (this latter too inclined to historicize).

3. There is a difficulty only in the case of *R̥V* 6,51,11 and 10,53,4–5, where the "five lands" are situated in heaven. But this is perhaps no more than a stylistic consequence of the fact that even though the cardinal points are made use of on earth, they are nonetheless identifiable only by celestial reference points (course of the sun; stars); cf. the theory of the round hearth and the square, oriented hearth in India and Rome, Dumézil, *Archaic Roman Religion*, trans. Philip Krapp (Chicago, 1970), pp. 312–19.

4. Despite Lüders, it is certainly not a question here of the zenith, which only later comes to be considered as the fifth direction.

5. Mircea Eliade, *Le Sacré et le profane* (1965), pp. 21–59, "L'espace sacré," with bibliography.

6. There is already an allusion in one of the *gāθās*: *Yasna* 32,3.

7. *Les types du premier homme et du premier roi dans l'histoire légendaire des Iraniens*, I (1917), pp. 117–18. One will find there the references to the Pahlavi texts. In the *Greater Bundahišn*, 14,36 and 18,9 (ed. Anklesaria), pp. 134 and 158, mentioning the emigration of the nine races on the back of the Ox, the six peripheral *kišvars* which they inhabit are still mythical worlds.

8. This impression is reinforced by a consideration of the *rat* (Avestan *ratu*, "protector spirit, president"), *Greater Bundahišn*, 29,2 (ed. Anklesaria), p. 252, borrowed from the list of names furnished by the *Yašt* of the Fravaši (Christensen, I, p. 121): the *rats* of the pair of northern *kišvars* have two names both ending in *-(a)spa*; those of the pair of southern *kišvars* are both sons of the same father.

9. One may also possibly detect the same influence upon the structure of the "seven priviliged clans" of the Achaemenids, which one rediscovers among the Arsacids and then the Sassanids; Arthur Christensen, *L'Iran sous les Sassanides* (1936), pp. 13–14 (Achaem.), 16,18 (Ars.), 98,101–2 (Sass.). Cf., in the theology, the passage in the number of Aməša Spəntas from six to seven by the incorporation of Ahura Mazdā, or of Ātar (Fire), or of Sraoša, or of Vərəθragna (Yazata of victory: see Dumézil, *The Destiny of the Warrior*, trans. Alf Hiltebeitel [Chicago, 1970], pp. 118–21, after Father Jean de Menasce); cf. Christensen, I, p. 192 and n. 1

10. *Celtic Heritage* (1961), chap. 5, "A Hierarchy of Provinces," pp. 118–19; chap.

6, "Involutions," pp. 140–45; chap. 7, "The Center," pp. 146–72; chap. 8, "Five Peaks" (in Wales), pp. 173–85.

11. Ibid., pp. 123–33.

12. "The Settling of the Manor of Tara," ed. and trans. R. I. Best, *Ériu* 4 (1910): 121–72. The words of Fontan are on pp. 144–60 (145–61 trans.). The scene is supposed to have taken place in the sixth century of our era, under the reign of Diarmait, son of Cerball.

13. A. and B. Rees compare this—shifting each term one direction counterclockwise, and replacing the *śūdras* by the musicians—with the ideal plan which the *Kauṭilya-Arthaśāstra* (trans. R. Shamasastry [Bangalore, 1915], pp. 60–61) gives of a royal fortress: in the center, slightly to the north of a site reserved for the gods and the sacrifice, the place of the king; around this, the priests to the north, the warriors to the east, the tiller-breeders to the south, the *śūdras* to the west.

14. Edward W. Hopkins, *Epic Mythology* (1915), pp. 149–52 (§91–92), on the *lokapālas* in the epic. There are instances where Indra, probably as king of the gods, may be removed from the list and replaced (in the north) by Soma, and the presence of this "sacrificial god" may have involved that of Agni, sometimes substituted for Kubera (in the east). The interpretation given in the text presumes that the canonical conception (V., I., Y., K.) was formed in a period when the functional value of the first two gods (sovereign, warrior) was still understood. Later the interpretations were of course different, for example that cited by Hopkins, p. 150, where the qualities conferred by each of the *lokapālas* upon the ideal "first king" are greatness (I.), restraint (Y.), beauty (V.), and wealth (K.).

15. Arthur Christensen, "Trebrödre- og Tobrödre-Stamsagn," *Danske Studier* (1916), p. 56.

16. *Herodotus* 4, 5–7. Most recently, see the discussion in my *Mythe et épopée* I, pp. 446–52.

17. *The Book of Conquests* (*Lebor Gabala Érenn*, IV = *Irish Texts Society*, 41 [1941], 28, §295), describing the occupation of Ireland by the Fir Bolg, shows them apportioning the island into five provinces (for there are five brothers), but disembarking with the invading army divided in three; it does not seem that these five provinces coincide exactly with the usual *cóiceds* (they are all on the periphery, but the two Munsters count only for one); see Françoise Le Roux, "La mythologie irlandaise du Livre des Conquêtes," *Ogam* 20 (1968): 329 and nn. 54–59. The traditions on the origin and the synthetic character of the central *cóiced* are of another type; they have been studied by F. Le Roux on pp. 168–76 of "Le Celticum d'Ambigatus et l'omphalos gaulois," *Ogam* 13 (1961): 158–84, as a sequel to Christian Guyanvarc'h, "Mediolanum Biturigum," ibid., pp. 137–58.

18. *Germania* 2,3: "celebrant carminibus antiquis, quod unum apud illos memoriae et annalium genus est, Tuistonem (variants: *Th-*, *Tr-*; *-sc-*, *-sb-*) deum terra editum et filium Mannum originem gentis, conditoresque Manno tres filios adsignant e quorum nominibus proximi Oceano Ingaevones, medii, Herminones, ceteri, Istaevones vocentur." *Tuisto* is certainly "the Twin" or "the Double" (cf. the Indo-Iranian *Yama*, the old-Icelandic *Ymir*). The trifunctional interpretation of his three grandsons was proposed as early as 1939 in my *Mythes et dieux des Germains*, p. 12, n. 1; see Jan de Vries, *Altgermanische Religionsgeschichte*, 2d ed., I (1956), p. 486; II (1957), p. 35. The individual proper names which one must suppose at the origin of the ethnic groups are not common names for gods, but their surnames: this is probably due to the source being poetic, *carmina*. The

first name *Inguia-, which refers to an individual god (if one may judge from the Scandinavian parallel), points us toward a similar interpretation for the two others; *Ermina- thus designates a god, and in Scandinavia only Óðinn receives the surname *jörmunr*, whatever may be the other usages of the word (notably as the first term of a compound); see the proposals of Jan de Vries, "La valeur religieuse du mot germanique *Irmin*," *Cahiers du Sud* 36 (1952), no. 314, pp. 18–27.

19. Franz-Rolf Schröder, *Ingunar-Freyr* (1941), esp. pp. 25–33.

20. Stig Wikander, *Der arische Männerbund* (1938), pp. 58–60.

21. The first function is thus in the middle (3,1,2), just as Oðinn is between Þórr and Freyr in the temple of Uppsala described by Adam of Bremen (2,1,3). A similar instance occurs in the division, by altitude, of the three functional families of heroes in the epic of the Ossetes: the Strong are at the summit of the mountains of the Narts, the Wise at the midway point, and the Rich at the foot (2,1,3), *Mythe et épopée* I, p. 456. Plato's *Republic*, which contains at the end of the third and the beginning of the fourth book such remarkable expositions of the tripartite ideology (cf. *Mythe et épopée* I, pp. 493–96), cannot be left out here (4, 435e–436[a], Francis M. Cornford, trans., *The Republic of Plato* [New York and London, 1945], p. 132): "Surely, I began [says Socrates], we must admit that the same elements and characters that appear in the state must exist in every one of us; where else could they come from? It would be absurd that among peoples with a reputation for a high spirited character (τὸ θυμοειδές), like the Thracians and the Scythians and northerners generally, the states have not derived that character from the individual members; or that it is otherwise with the love of knowledge (τὸ φιλομαθές) which would be ascribed chiefly to our part of the world, or with the love of money (τὸ φιλοχρηματόν), which one would specially connect with Phoenecia and Egypt."

22. "Le partage du monde dans la tradition iranienne," *Journal Asiatique* 240 (1952): 455–63. On all this, see *Mythe et épopée* I, pp. 586–88, "Le choix." Molé emphasized, against the opinion of Minorsky, that the functional division in the legend is not secondary (*Mythe et épopée* I, p. 586, n. 2).

23. That of the *Āyātkar i Jāmāspik*, a Pahlavi text reconstituted on the basis of a Parsee transcription (Messina). In another variant (Ferdowsi), Feridūn dons a frightful disguise and observes the behavior of his three sons—cowardice, temerity, and reasoned courage—according to which he allots them their portions.

24. Marijan Molé, *La légende de Zoroastre selon les textes Pehlevis* (1967), p. 157 (note to *Dēnkart* VII,2,1): "Without doubt, the translation of *xvarnah* by 'glory' is to be abandoned; but if the term is derived from the root *ar-*, 'to obtain,' its signification is not simply that of 'fortune.' It is actually a question of the 'lot' attributed to each person in order that he may accomplish his task. This meaning, at once greater and more precise than that postulated by M. Bailey, takes account of all the uses of the term, notably of its quasi-equivalence with *xvēškārīh*, cf. *Culte, mythe et cosmologie*, 434ff." My own preference is to maintain the use of "glory"; the explanation by *ar-* is very improbable.

25. *Mbh.* I,83–85, śl. 3424–3534 (Calc.); 78–80 (Poona). The story of Yayāti in the first book of the *Mahābhārata* is a composite text. In particular, it comprises a variant that shows little compatibility with what is analyzed here: during his fall, Yayāti teaches Aṣṭaka that reincarnation is brought on by a natural exhaustion of merits, not by a posthumous sin. As J. A. B. van Buitenen has shown ("Some Notes on the *Uttara-Yāyāta*," *Adyar Library* [volume in honor of V. Raghavan,

[1968], pp. 617–35), this teaching corresponds, even verbally, with the doctrine exposed in several Upaniṣads, notably the fifth book of the *Chāndogya*: "bardic literature" making use of "baronial lore."

26. *Mbh.* I,83,3462.

27. Ibid., 3463.

28. Ibid., 3464.

29. One naturally thinks of the violent discussion in *Alcestes* between Admetis and his son who refuses to die in his place.

30. *Mbh.* I,84,3468–69, 3475–76, 3482–83, 3488, 3492–93.

31. Ibid., 3470–73.

32. Ibid., 3477.

33. Ibid., 3484.

34. Ibid., 3489.

35. Ibid., 3474, 3478–80, 3486–87, 3490–91.

36. On this interpretation of *bhoja*, see D. B. Kosambi, "The Vedic 'Five Tribes'" (n. 2 above), p. 28.

37. Like the promotion of Ērič at the expense of his seniors (see above), that of Pūru does not occur without protests, *Mbh.* I,85,3518–31.

38. *Mbh.* I,85,3433 (Poona, 80,20).

39. See below, n. 57.

40. See the most recent discussions in B. Schlerath and D. B. Kosambi, referred to in n. 2 above.

41. "Über die Liedverfasser des Rigveda, nebst Bemerkungen über die vedische Chronologie und über die Geschichte des Rituals," *Zeitschrift der deutschen morgenländischen Gesellschaft* 42(1888): 199–247.

42. It should be noted that these four names are those of the four sons whom the epic Yayāti sends out to the periphery; probably in Vedic times they corresponded to the four directions as opposed to the center (where the invoking priest is placed); see above, n. 4.

43. What follows is taken, with several changes, from my *Mythes et dieux des Germains*, pp. 57–60.

44. "König Aun in Upsala und Kronos," *Festskrift til Hjalmar Falk* (1927), pp. 245–61.

45. A Norwegian tradition probably contains the same belief in an attenuated form (G. Vigfusson and C. R. Unger, eds., *Flateyjarbók* 1 [1860]: 24): "When Halfdan the Old took over the kingdom (*a et hann tók konungdom*), he made a great sacrifice in mid-winter in order to be able to live for three hundred years in his kingdom (*til þess at hann skyldi mega lifa. ccc. vetra konongdómi sínum*); it was answered to him that he himself would live no more than one life of man (*ecki meirr enn einn mannzaldr*) but that his race would remain brilliant for three hundred years." We do not know what he sacrificed on this occasion, but what follows is at least mystically equivalent to the "sacrifice" of Aun: it seems that it was at the expense of his first nine sons that Halfdan had obtained the collective good fortune of his race. In fact, it is said that these first nine sons died in battle, all at the same age, leaving no heirs (*suá er sagt at engi þeirra ætti börn ok fellu allir senn í orrostu*), and the prophesy was accomplished through a second series of nine sons and through their descendants. There is no reason to think that the story of Halfdan was borrowed from that of Aun or vice versa: the two are varied historicizations of a common belief.

46. Trace of a hierarchy in which Shem is dominant.

47. Cf. Ezekiel 5,5: "This is Jerusalem; I have set her in the center of the nations, with countries round about her" (cited by Schlerath [above, n. 2], p. 32, referring to Wilhelm Roscher, *Omphalos*, pp. 24–25, on the "kingdom of the middle" among the Hebrews).

48. It is even more interesting to see the biblical account endowed in the Middle Ages with a trifunctional value in connection with the "three estates" (*oratores, bellatores, laboratores,* etc.). Jacques le Goff has pointed up this usage in his important article, "Note sur la société tripartie: idéologie monarchique et renouveau économique de la chrétienté du IXe au XIIe siècle," *L'Europe aux IXe–XIe siècles,* Colloque de Varsovie, 1965 (1968), pp. 63–71; we read on p. 63, n. 2: "D. Treštík has rightly called attention to the importance of the text of *Genesis* (9,18–27), in the treatment of the theme of the tripartite society in medieval literature (*Československý Časopis Historický* [1964], p. 453). The curse cast by Noah on his son Ham to the advantage of his brothers Shem and Japhet (*Maledictus Chanaan, seruus seruorum erit fratribus suis*) was utilized by the medieval authors to define the relations between the two superior orders and the third, subordinated order. But the exploitation of this text seems relatively late."

49. The beginning of a functional interpretation, which limited itself to establishing the children of the "good son" in the first function. It is picturesque to see the Jewish people forgotten in this declaration of "Semite" racism.

50. Chaps. 41 (story of the prophet Noah) and 42 (story of Dho^chāk), from the translation of Hermann Zotenberg, I (1867), pp. 114–16.

51. *Mbh.* V,5046–48:

> yādavānāṃ kulakaro balavān vīryasaṃmataḥ
> avamene sa tu kṣatraṃ darpapūrṇaḥ sumandadhīḥ.
> na cātiṣṭhat pituḥ śāstre baladarpavimohitaḥ
> avamene ca pitaraṃ bhrātr̥̄ṃś cāpy aparājitaḥ.
> pr̥thivyāṃ caturantāyāṃ yadur evābhavad balī
> vaśe kr̥tvā sa nr̥patīn avasan nāgasāhvaye.

52. Ibid., V,5049:

> taṃ pitā paramakruddho yayātir nahuṣātmajaḥ
> śaśāpa putraṃ gāndhāre rājyāc ca vyapāropayat.

53. Ibid., 5050:

> ye cainam anvavartanta bhrātaro baladarpitam
> śaśāpa tān api kruddho yayātis tanayān atha.

54. Ibid., 5052:

> yavīyāṃsaṃ tataḥ pūruṃ putraṃ svavaśavartinam
> rājye niveśayām āsa vidheyaṃ nr̥pasattamaḥ.

(*rājya* is at once both "kingship" and "kingdom".)

55. *Mbh.* V,148,5042–52.

56. It should be pointed out that the variant of the fifth book does not raise the (theoretical!) difficulty that is met in the first with regard to the given facts concerning time: in this latter, Śarmiṣṭhā's sons (and certainly their half-brothers also) are still small boys when their carelessness draws upon their father the curse of their grandfather; but as soon as the curse has had its effect (an immediate one), they converse with their father like young men of experience.

57. *Mbh.* I,87,3555. In place of *antya-* ("that which is at the extremity on the boundary, peripheral"), Poona I,82,4 gives *anta-* ("end, border, limit"), a variant

of the same sense. In fact, despite this beautiful declaration opposing the center to the periphery, the countries where the four bad sons are sent seem to be concentrated in the northwest. This probably is related to displacements of peoples and changes in their horizon between the time of the hymns and that of the epic (Kosambi, see n. 2 above, pp. 38–39). This *śloka* thus prolongs the old doctrine, while *śloka* 3533 (above, n. 38) "actualizes" the doctrine geographically in an inadequate, degenerate fashion.

Chapter 2

1. See chap. 4, sec. 3.
2. *Mbh.* V,118,4023.
3. Originally, according to a variant, *Vasumat*, "the man provided with material goods."
4. *Mbh.* V,115,3954.
5. Ibid., V,119,4037–47.
6. Ibid., I,87–88,3551–66.
7. Ibid., I,3555; see above, chap. 1, n. 57.
8. Ibid., I,119,4053–55.
9. Ibid., I,88,3567–68.
10. Ibid., V,119,4055–56.
11. Ibid., V,4057–60.

    4057: caturo 'paśyata nr̥pāṃs teṣāṃ madhye papāta ha
    pratardano vasumanāḥ śibir auśīnaro 'ṣṭakaḥ.

12. Ibid., I,88,3569.
13. Ibid., V,119,4060–62.
14. Ibid., V,120,4078.
15. Ibid., V,120,4080.
16. Ibid., I,92–93,3653, 3656, 3664, 3668.
17. Ibid., I,3673—a hell that is "terrestrial, on earth," not "subterranean"; J. A. B. van Buitenen (see chap. 1, n. 25) has recognized the doctrine of *saṃsāra*, "transmigration," here.
18. *Mbh.* I,3675–79.
19. Ibid., 3683–87.

    sarvām imāṃ pr̥thivīṃ nirjigāya
    preṣṭhe(?) baddhvā hy adadaṃ brāhmaṇebhyaḥ
    medhyān aśvān ekaśaphān surūpāṃs
    tadā devāḥ puṇyabhājo bhavanti
    adām ahaṃ pr̥thivīṃ brāhmaṇebhyaḥ
    pūrṇām imām akhilāṃ vāhanasya
    gobhiḥ suvarṇena dhanaiś ca mukhyais
    tatrāsan gāḥ śatam arbudāni
    satyena me dyauś ca vasuṃdharā ca
    tathaivāgnir jvalate mānuṣeṣu . . .

20. Ibid., V,119,4066–67.
21. Ibid., 4068–77.
22. Ibid., 120,4078–79.
23. Ibid., V,120,4081–83.
24. Ibid., 4083–85.

25. Ibid., 4085–89.
26. Ibid., 4089–92.
27. Ibid., I,93,3680.
28. Ibid., 3681–82.
29. See chap. 4, sec. 1.
30. See above, n. 19.
31. Here the Calcutta edition interpolates a verse rightly rejected by the Poona edition.
32. satyena me dyauśca vasuṃdharā ca
tathaivāgnir jvalate mānuṣeṣu
na me vṛthā vyāhṛtam eva vākyaṃ
satyaṃ hi santaḥ pratipūjayanti.
[. . .]
sarve ca devā munayaś ca lokāḥ
satyena pūjyā iti me manogatam.
33. Pahlavi *Yam, Yam-šēt* (see Introduction, p. 4); from here on, the reader is permanently referred to Arthur Christensen's *Les types du premier homme*, II (see Introduction, n. 7).
34. See Introduction.
35. See chap. 1, n. 24.
36. Christensen, II, p. 13.
37. Ibid., 23.
38. Ibid., p. 69.
39. gar īdūn ki dān-īd ki man kard-am īn
ma-rā xᵛān bāy-ad ǰahān-afarīn.
40. Reuben Levy, trans., *The Epic of Kings: Shāh-nāma* (Chicago, 1967), pp. 10–11; Christensen, p. 103.
41. From Hermann Zotenberg, ed., p. 16.
42. Christensen, II, p. 14.
43. Cf. my *Destiny of the Warrior*, pp. 130–31. On the essential relations between the *xᵛarənah* and Vərəθrağna, the genius of victory, see E. Benveniste [and L. Renou], *Vṛtra-Vṛθrağna* (1934), pp. 7, 31, 49–50. The bird Vārəğna, i.e., the falcon (Benveniste, p. 34), is justly one of Vərəθrağna's incarnations.
44. *Zend Avesta*, II (1892), p. 625, n. 52.
45. Christensen, II, p. 53.
46. *Zend Avesta*, II, p. 625, n. 55; moreover, Ferīdūn's famous club is in the form of a bull's head.
47. *The Destiny of the Warrior*, p. 18; Marijan Molé has independently made the same comparison and has developed it in his later books.
48. Taken from Molé's translation, *La légende de Zoroastre*, pp. 9 and 11 (text, pp. 8 and 10), cf. the study, pp. 242–49; the text cited (p. 242) from the *Dātastān i Dēnīk*, 37,35 implies, by the bringing together of three names, another list, with another titulary for the first function. Between two references to the complete *xvarrah* appear Frētōn, Manuščihr, and Karsāsp (Ošnar only coming after): "[Several perfect ones will be born: . . .] he who will be full of *xvarrah*, Yam: he who will be a healer [*pur-bēšāz*], Frētōn; he who will be endowed with two wisdoms [*har 2-xrat*], Manuščihr; he who will be very strong [*pur-ōǰ*] Karsāsp; he who will be from a race endowed with *xvarrah*, Kai Kavāt." The order of the functions is most satisfactory in the *Dēnkart*: 3,2,1 (*Yašt* 19:1,3,2; *Dāt. i Dēnīk*: 3,1,2).

49. The sole problem is to explain the improprieties—there are three—in the text of *Yašt* 19, which is less satisfactory than the *Dēnkart* but rests on the same tradition. One may glimpse the cause of the first and the second, namely the complete effacement of any characteristic of the third function (agriculture, medicine, etc.) in the presentation of Θraētaona, who, without nuance, retains and proclaims only his quality of being "victorious"; and, in the second place, the incongruity made by the symmetrical placing, as beneficiaries of the three flights of the x^v*arənah*, of a god (one of the greatest) and two mortals. (1) This text is inserted in a Yašt which, nominally consecrated to the Earth, is in fact the "Yašt of the x^v*arənah*." Passing from one hero to another, the x^v*arənah* is taken there for what it is generally, a pledge of divine election for victory (see above, chap. 1, n. 24), and in other verses no allusion is made to other results or manifestations of divine election besides victory. It is thus comprehensible that Θraētaona, whom the tradition placed here with a more complex justification, has been simplified and reduced if not to the type, then at least to the level of Kərəsāspa, the one being "the most victorious of the victorious," the other "the strongest of strong men." (2) It is equally comprehensible that "the being of the first function" called upon by the structure would also have been oriented toward victory and not chosen, for example, only for his wisdom or science or for his pacific or even bureaucratic institutions. Miθra meets this need: incontestably "sovereign," the very highest of the Yazatas, and still partly charged with what constituted the province (justice, law) of the Indo-Iranian sovereign god *Mitra, he is at the same time, as a result of the Zoroastrian reform, one of the heirs and substitutes of the eliminated Indra: god of combat (of good combat, of the crusade), armed with the *vaẓra* like the Indian Indra with the *vajra*, a god for whom the specialist of victory Vərəθrağna is only the auxiliary. (3) In return, one does not find an explanation for the third impropriety, the series of ordinal expressions ("first," "second," "third" x^v*arənah*) which stands opposed to the much more satisfactory notion of a "division" (*baxšišn*) of one unique *xvarrah* which is found in the *Dēnkart*. On the one hand, it is unthinkable that Yima would have possessed three x^v*arənahs* all at once. On the other hand, his sin being unique and exhaustive in all the texts of every epoch, there is no reason to suppose that, at a more ancient point in the tradition, he had sinned three times and that, pardoned twice, he had been definitively punished only after the final relapse. See below, pp. 110–12.

50. Such is the story in the texts of the Muslim period. The Avestan texts are silent on the scene of the sin.

51. See chap. 2, sec. 2.

52. Ibid. Ancient Ireland presents a remarkable correspondence with India (and the Indo-Iranians) with regard to the exaltation of the Truth and the marvelous effects of the "truth of the king"; see Myles Dillon, *The Archaism of Irish Tradition: Reprints in Irish Studies*, from the American Committee for Irish Studies (University of Chicago), 5 (1969), reprinted from the *Proceedings of the British Academy* 33 (1947): 4–5.

53. See above, n. 32.

54. See chap 2, sec. 3.

55. *Mythe et épopée* I, p. 618, citing Kaj Barr, *Avesta* (1954), pp. 35–36; see chap. 3, sec. 3.

56. This essential reduction to the lie of other forms of Yima's sin (pride, revolt against God, even "the desire to know more than God had revealed to him) is

well marked in the passage of the Pahlavi *Rivāyat* translated by Molé, *La légende de Zoroastre*, pp. 248–49; it is added there: "Whoever boasts of qualities he does not have, those which he does have will leave him as they left Yam"; cf. p. 256, *Dātistān i Dēnīk*, 39, 16–17 ("lie," *druǰišn*).

57. See Introduction.

58. See chap. 1, sec. 2.

59. *Yasna* 19, 16–17, is alone in mentioning the *huītiš*, artisans, as a fourth term.

60. J. Darmesteter, *Zend Avesta*, II, p. 27, n. 53; E. Benveniste, "Les classes sociales dans la tradition avestique," *Journal Asiatique* 221 (1932): 119–20; cf. *Mythe et épopée* I, p. 525.

61. "La préhistoire . . ." (see above, Intro., n. 11), pp. 109–30; Benveniste, "Les classes . . ." (see above, Intro., n. 11), p. 119. Cf. *Greater Bundahišn* 18,10 (ed. Anklesaria), p. 118: Yam makes everything during his reign with the aid of the three functional fires; cf. the trifunctional designation of Yima (*Yašt* 13,130): *ašaonō yimahe sūrahe pouru.vąθwahe*, "of Yima, true to Order, strong, rich in herds."

62. See chap. 1, sec. 4 (end).

63. On Kāvya Uśanas, see *Mythe et épopée* II, part 2.

64. See Ibid., pp. 194–96.

65. From Christensen's translation, II, p. 12, where parallel texts are given.

66. Ibid., p. 69.

67. Hermann Zotenberg, trans., *Chronique, Persian version by Belʿamī*, I (1867), p. 179; Christensen, II, p. 86. Cf. Yam's boasts in the Pahlavi *Rivāyat* (Molé, *La Légende de Zoroastre*, p. 248): "And he affirmed: 'It is I who have created the water, it is I who have created the earth . . . (etc., etc.).' Thus he lied, knowing only the fact that he was the creator, but ignoring how he had created."

68. H. Zotenberg, I, p. 63; Christensen, p. 88.

69. See chap. 2, sec. 5.

70. Christensen, I, pp. 109–23; Molé, p. 147.

71. Christensen, I, pp. 14–16.

72. Yima acts not through his own power, but as delegated by God: cf. *Dēnkart*, VII, 1, 21–23 (Molé, pp. 6–8; tr. 7–9).

73. The most likely interpretation is that of Sir Harold W. Bailey, *Zoroastrian Problems in the Ninth-Century Books* (1943), pp. 219–24.

74. At a time when the various peoples that had sprung from the Indo-Europeans were more mobile, in particular during the migrations, there must have existed an even greater folklore of population displacements treated as the consequence of conflicts between age groups. Cf. the legends which recount the abolition of the custom of killing the aged, and which sometimes end up with the emigration of the young: for example, in Saxo Grammaticus, VIII, 12–13, Aggo and Ebbo decide in the course of a famine not to massacre the *senes invalidos* as had been decided (*plebiscito provisum est*), but to lead the *robustiores* abroad—from which come the people of the Lombards (*Mythes et dieux des Germains*, chap. 5, "Conflits d'âges et migrations," pp. 73–75). Cf. in Italy, Romulus and Remus founding Rome in order to allow their grandfather, who had been restored by their efforts, to rule in Alba.

Chapter 3

1. *Mbh.*, 1,63,2334–419.

2. Janamejaya is the son of Parikṣit, son of Abhimanyu, son of Arjuna.

3. *Mythe et épopée* I, pp. 178–82.
4. The geneological table:

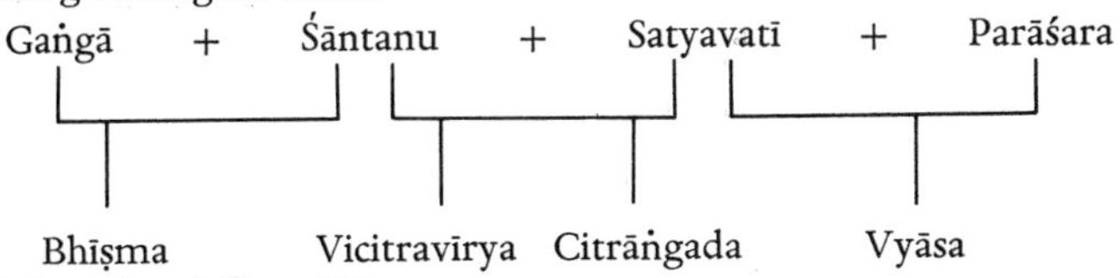

See *Mythe et épopée* II, p. 238.

5. Arthur Christensen, *Les types du premier homme* I, pp. 109–23; *Greater Bundahišn*, (ed. Anklesaria), pp. 126–34.

6. See above, n. 1.

7. This festival has occasioned many studies; most recently with bibliography (notably a just appreciation of Johann Jakob Meyer, *Trilogie altindischer Mächte und Feste der Vegetation* [1937]), Jan Gonda, "The Indra Festival According to the Atharvavedin," *Journal of the American Oriental Society* 87 (1967): 413–29, who insists on the royal character of the ceremony.

8. It is he who inherits the chariot, *Mbh.* 2,23,950; he will transmit it to Jarāsandha, on whom see *Mythe et épopée* II, pp. 96–108.

9. See above, chap. 1, secs. 2–4.

10. *Mbh.* 13,115,5647–52. For the very similar problems among the Pythagoreans, see Marcel Détienne, "La cuisine de Pythagore," *Archives de Sociologie Religieuse*, no. 29 (1960), pp. 141–62 (rich bibliography).

11. *Mbh.* 12,339,12818–58. On the speculations concerning the cosmic *aja*, see my "Notes sur le bestiaire cosmique de l'Edda et du R̥gVeda," *Mélanges Fernand Mossé* (1959), pp. 104–12; and on the substitution of plant for animal offerings, Sylvain Lévi, *La doctrine du sacrifice dans les Brāhmaṇas* (1898, repr. 1966), pp. 136–38.

12. *Mbh.* 14,91,2818–31.

13. *yathopanītair yaṣṭavyam*, 2830.

14. See chap. 2, sec. 2.

15. Hopkins, *Epic Mythology*, §69 (Indra's *dhvaja*, *ketu*), pp. 125–26: "If it is impossible to bring 'Indra's day' into connection with Indra's festival, it is at least clear that the festival occurred after the rains had ceased and when New Year's was celebrated, for in its installation it is especially said that the feast takes place at the end of the year, *gate saṃvatsare*." But this latter expression could mean simply: "When a year had passed after the event, the anniversary of the event."

16. H. Zotenberg, pp. 179–80; Christensen, *Les Types du premier homme* (see above, chap. 2, n. 66), II, p. 86.

17. Zotenberg, pp. 13–14; Christensen, II, p. 97.

18. Sochau edition, pp. 216, 220; Christensen, II, p. 99.

19. From J. Mohl, ed. and trans., I (1838), p. 52; Christensen, II, p. 103. On the variants of the tradition of the Muslim epoch, see Christensen, II, p. 114, n. 2, and the excursus on "le Nowrōz," pp. 138–60.

20. See chap. 2, sec. 3; Christensen, II, pp. 13–14.

21. Christensen, II, p. 11.

22. *Zoroastre* (1948), p. 255, cf. pp. 42–43; Duchesne-Guillemin's translation is rendered into English by M. Henning, tr., *The Hymns of Zarathustra* (1952), p. 121. Another, less likely, translation makes Yima himself eat the flesh of the ox.

23. Christensen, II, pp. 21, 49. Cf. the text of the metrical Säddär, cited by Christensen, II, p. 94. In India, it occurs that Vasu Uparicara is characterized by his refusal of bloody sacrifices, thus *Mbh.* 12,338,12760–61 (with respect to a great sacrifice celebrated by him): "There was no slaughter of animals there, and that through the king's decision, as he was against violence," *na tatra paśughāto 'bhūt sa rājaivāsthito 'bhavat | ahiṃsraḥ* . . . ; cf. the text of Ferdowsi, cited by Christensen, II, p. 49.

24. There are naturally other legends about the first (guilty) consumption of butchered food. The *Greater Bundahišn*, 14,21–31 (ed. Anklesaria), pp. 130–32, attributes it to Mašya and Mašyānī. But as Christensen remarks (II, pp. 48–49): "Mašya and Mašyānī do not introduce among men the custom of eating animal flesh (§21); they eat it themselves, and their nature thereby becomes more gross" (they even end up eating their first pair of children, §31), while "Yima is the one who teaches men to eat meat."

25. See chap. 2 and n. 73.

26. *Dātistān i Dēnīk*, 39,18; Christensen, II, p. 23: ". . . and he obtained his pardon from the Creator, who is endowed with an absolute existence, and he spoke to his successors and gave them warnings (?) relative to the retribution reserved for those who abandon the Creator's service." According to a Persian poem (ibid., p. 73), J̌imšed, after his death, suffered two thousand years in hell close by the *dēv* Satan; then, in response to the prayer of Zoroaster, God made him pass for a thousand years into purgatory, and finally into the paradise of the Just, "where he was joyous and happy."

27. See "Perspectives," for another consideration (concerning rituals).

Chapter 4

1. *Mbh.* V,105–19,3718–4046.
2. *Mythe et épopée* I, pp. 532–36.
3. *Mbh.* V,105,3739–40:

> nirbahdhatas tu bahuśo gālavasya tapasvinaḥ
> kiñcid āgatasaṃrambho viśvāmitro 'bravīd idam.
> ekataḥ śyāmakarṇānāṃ hayānāñ candravarcasām
> aṣṭau śatāni me dehi gaccha gālava mā ciram.

Cf., in the ancient Celtic world, in Ireland as well as in Wales, the white cows with red ears, often mentioned (demanded, offered) as exceptionally precious animals. Osborn Bergin, *Ériu* 14 (1940–46): 170.

4. *Mbh.* V,113,3904:

> vibhavaś cāsya sumahān āsīd dhanapater iva
> evaṃ gurudhanaṃ vidvan dānenaiva viśodhaya.

5. *Mbh.* V,118,3929–30:

> asyāṃ śulkaṃ pradāsyanti nr̥pā rājyam api dhruvam
> kiṃ punaḥ śyāmakarṇānāṃ dve catuḥśate.
> sa bhavān pratigr̥hṇātu mamaitāṃ mādhavīṃ sutām
> ahaṃ dauhitravān syāṃ vai vara eṣa mama prabho.

6. Ibid., 113,3932:

> upalabdham idaṃ dvāram aśvānām iti cāṇḍajaḥ.

7. Ibid., 113,3936–37:

> kanyeyaṃ mama rājendra prasavaiḥ kulavardhinī.

iyaṃ śulkena bhāryārthaṃ haryaśva pratigṛhyatām
śulkaṃ te kīrtayiṣyāmi tat śrutvā saṃpradhāryatām.

8. The six elevated parts are: the two bosoms, the two hips, the two eyes (there are variants); the seven delicate: skin, hair, teeth, fingers, toes, waist, neck; the three deep: navel, voice, intelligence; the five red: the palms, the outer corners of the eyes, tongue, lips, and palate (here too there are variants).

9. *Mbh.* V,114,3940–41:

bahulakṣaṇasampannā bahuprasavadhāriṇī
samartheyaṃ janayituñ cakravartinam ātmajam.

10. *Mbh.* V,114,3946:

so 'ham ekam apatyaṃ vai janayiṣyāmi gālava
asyām etaṃ bhavān kāmaṃ sampādayatu me varam.

11. *Mbh.* V,114,3949–50:

nṛpebhyo hi caturbhyas te pūrṇāny aṣṭau śatāni me
bhaviṣyanti t^ thā putrā mama catvāra eva ca.
kriyatām upasaṃhāro gurvartho dvijasattama.

12. *Mbh.* V,114,3952:

iyaṃ kanyā naraśrestha haryaśva pratigṛhyatām
caturbhāgena śulkasya janayasvaikam ātmajam.

13. See above, chap. 2, sec. 1.

14. *Mbh.* V,114,3956:

jāto nṛpa sutas te 'yam bālo bhāskarasannibhaḥ
kālo gantuṃ naraśreṣṭha bhikṣārtham aparaṃ nṛpam.

15. *Mbh.* V,114,3958: *kumarī kāmato bhūtvā.*

16. *Mbh.* V,115,3979:

niryātayatu me kanyāṃ bhavāṃs tiṣthantu vājinaḥ
yāvad anyatra gacchāmi śulkārthaṃ pṛthivīpate.

17. *Mbh.* V,116,3992:

aham apy ekam evāsyāṃ janayiṣyāmi gālava
putraṃ dvija gataṃ mārgaṃ gamiṣyāmi parair aham.

18. *Mbh.* V,117,4004–11.

19. *Mbh.* V,117,4014–15:

asyāṃ rājarṣibhiḥ putrā jātā vai dhārmikās trayaḥ
caturthaṃ janayatv ekaṃ bhavān api narottamam.
pūrṇāny evam śatāny aṣṭau turagānāṃ bhavantu te
bhavato hy anṛṇo bhūtvā tapaḥ kuryāṃ yathāsukham.

20. *Mbh.* V,117,4017–18:

kim iyaṃ pūrvam eveha na dattā mama gālava
putrā mamaiva catvāro bhaveyuḥ kulabhāvanāḥ,
pratigṛhṇāmi te kanyām ekaputraphalāya vai
aśvāś cāśramam āsādya carantu mama sarvaśaḥ.

21. *Mbh.* V,117,4023:

jāto dānapatiḥ putras tvayā śūras tathā 'paraḥ
satyadharmaratas cānyo yajvā cāpi tathā paraḥ.

22. *Mbh.* V,117,4025.

23. *Mbh.* V,118,4026–36.

24. See chap. 2, sec. 2.

25. See chap. 4, sec. 1.

26. See *Mythe et épopée* II, p. 220.

27. As with so many other legends taken from pre-Zoroastrian heroes, this one, *mutatis mutandis*, has been transported onto Zoroaster: adding the milk to the account of *Dēnkart* 7, 2, 14–35, Šarastānī writes (Molé, *La légende de Zoroastre*, p. 159): "He put the soul of Zoroaster into a tree and made it grow on the heights and surrounded it with seventy noble angels. They planted it on the summit of one of the mountains of the Azerbeijan which is called *Asnavandgar. Then he mixed Zoroaster's body with cow's milk. Zoroaster's father drank it. The milk first became sperm and then an embryo in his mother's womb. Satan attacked the embryo and made it suffer, but the mother heard a voice from heaven which gave her directions for its cure." Cf. Harold W. Bailey, *Zoroastrian Problems in the Ninth Century Books* (1943), p. 27, n. 2.

28. In classical Sanskrit, *mādhvī* subsists beside *mādhavī*, with the same meaning: "sort of alcohol"; "springtime flower." After hearing my lecture on Medb and Mādhavī, Akos Östör, a distinguished graduate of the University of Chicago who had spent a long time in West Bengal, presented me with the following note: "It is common knowledge that the Mahu (or colloquially Mau) flower causes intoxication. In the Bankura and Birbhum districts of West Bengal the flowers may be eaten raw or liquor may be distilled from the honey of these big flowers, in both cases the effect being much the same. The people also feed the flowers to cows to increase the cow's milk supply. The Mahua is a huge, spreading tree, its leaves are dark green, large and shiny. The flowers are very big and white. In English the tree is known as a kind of butter tree, the flower as the honey flower. There is a reference to these qualities of the flower in one of Tarashankar Bannerjee's novels. In a beautiful passage he invokes the effects of the Mahua flower (its relation to intoxication and milk) and thus creates an atmosphere of nostalgia. The novel is called "Ganadevota," it was published by Pearl Publications (Bombay, 1969, pp. 184–86). It was this passage that made me think of the connection with your argument about the charming Mādhavī. Later I found a reference in L. S. S. O'Malley's District Gazetteer of Bankura (1908) to the revenue gained by the government from the taxes on liquor made from the *mahua* flower. Distillation was quite an industry then." See also Irawati Karve, *Yugānta: The End of an Epoch* (Poona, 1969), pp. 141–42: "At present the central Indian forests contain a large beautiful tree called *Mahuva*. This tree, called *Madhuka* in Sanskrit, is a source of bounty for tribal people. From its leaves they make plates; from its fragrant honey-filled flowers they make wine. The dried blossoms are eaten as a delicacy, and from the sticky juice of the flowers all kinds of sweetmeats are made."

29. An original variant has recently been proposed for it by Jaan Puhvel, "Aspects of Equine Functionality," in *Myth and Law among the Indo-Europeans* (1970), p. 167.

Chapter 5

1. *Eochaid*, or *Eochu*, genitive *E(o)chach*. On this name (**ivocatus*, "who fights with the yew"), see note and bibliography of Françoise Le Roux, *Ogam* 20 (1968): 393, n. 60. (Jaan Puhvel, *Myth and Law* . . . [see above, chap. 4, n. 29], prefers to explain Eochaid by *ech*, "horse.") On principle, I conserve the orthography of each source.

2. The principal studies are: Tomás ó Máille, "Medb Cruachna," *Zeitschrift für Celtische Philologie* 17 (1928; volume dedicated to Thurneysen): 129–46; Rudolf

Thurneysen, "Göttin Medb?" ibid. 18 (1930): 108–10, and "Zur Göttin Medb," ibid. 19 (1931–33): 352–53 (aligning it with a Sumerian *hieros gamos*); Alexander Haggerty Krappe, "The Sovereignty of Erin," *The American Journal of Philology* 63 (1942): 444–54; Josef Weisweiler, *Heimat und Herrschaft, Wirkung und Ursprung eines irischen Mythos* (1943), notably chap. 6 ("die Herrschaft über Irland"), pp. 86–120 (esp. pp. 91–104); Alwyn and Brinley Rees, *Celtic Heritage* (1961), pp. 73–75; Françoise Le Roux-Guyonvarc'h, *Celticum* 15 (1966), pp. 339–50 of her commentary on the *Tochmare Etaine* (pp. 328–74, with etymological appendices by Christian Guyonvarc'h, pp. 377–84). What follows here summarizes, with T. ó Máille, the basic text, the *Cath Bóinde*, edited and translated by Joseph O'Neill, *Ériu* 2 (1905): 173 (introduction), 174–84 (text), 175–85 (translation).

3. O'Neill, pp. 176–77; ó Máille, pp. 130–31.

4. See Myles Dillon, "The Act of Truth in Celtic Tradition," *Modern Philology* 44 (1946–47): 140.

5. O'Neill, pp. 176–80, 177–81; ó Máille, pp. 131–33.

6. O'Neill, pp. 176–82, 177–83; ó Máille, p. 134.

7. O'Neill, pp. 182–84, 183–85; ó Máille, pp. 135–36.

8. Thurneysen, pp. 108–9.

9. *Táin Bó Cuailnge*, ed. Ernst Windisch (1905): (version of the Book of Leinster), p. 6 (p. 7, transl.). At the beginning of the *Táin*, Medb also enumerates the four suitors whom she eliminated in her preference for Ailill: as to these five, they represent the five Cóiceds of Ireland, as underlined by Windisch, pp. 4 and 5.

10. ó Máille, pp. 136–39, where all the references can be found.

11. *Esnada Tige Buchet*, ed. and tr. Whitley Stokes, *Revue Celtique* 25 (1904): 23 (p. 24, transl.); cf. p. 34, variant.

12. Maura Power, "Cnucha Cnoc os Cion Life," *Zeitschrift für Celtische Philologie* 11 (1917): 43 (p. 48, transl.), distich 30:

doratsat Laighin na lann righi do mac righ Eirenn.
nocor fhaidh Medb lesin mac nirbo righ Eirenn Cormac.

13. On Niall, I summarize: Standish Ó'Grady, *Silva Gadelica* (1892), I, pp. 326–30 (text), II, pp. 368–73 (transl.); Maud Joint, "Echtra Max Echdach Mugmedoin," Érin 4 (1910): 104–6; Whitley Stokes, [same title] *Revue Celtique* 24 (1903): 190–207; Krappe, pp. 448–49.

14. A little later she renames herself: "I am the Sovereignty of Ireland," *missi banflaith hErenn.*

15. On Lugaid, I summarize: the *Cóir Anman*, ed. Whitley Stokes, in *Irische Texte* III, 2 (1897), §70, pp. 316–22 (317–323, transl.); cf. Krappe, pp. 444–45, with the variant of the *Dinšenchas* in verse.

16. Krappe, pp. 447–48, suggests a connection between some Greek and Iranian traditions that should certainly be kept apart: for example, the ram in the story of Ardašīr is something else, one of the incarnations of Vərəθrağna, the spirit of victory—as is also the boar.

17. ó Máille, pp. 142–43; Weisweiler, p. 92.

18. For Niall's story, see above, sec. 2 and n. 13: "I am Sovereignty," said the ravishing girl, "and just as you have at first seen me ugly, sodden, and repugnant, and beautiful only at the end, so will it be with royal power: only in hard combats can it be won, but in the end he who is king shows himself gracious and noble," *Silva Gadelica* I, p. 329, II, p. 372; "Royalty is harsh (*garb*) at the beginning, sweet (*blaith*) in the middle, peaceable (*saim*) at the end," *Ériu* 4 (1910): 106; cf. *Revue*

Celtique 24 (1903): 200. Krappe misuses a poetic expression of Tha'alabī (ed. and tr. H. Zotenberg, p. 137), from which he artificially constructs a "tradition," in order to attribute a homologous legend to Iran: "[Zaw] had received the royalty from Afrāsyāb when it was like an old woman, ugly and toothless; he transmitted her to Kay Qobādh like a young bride"; the author simply notes, in his florid style, how the situation in Iran was ameliorated thanks to Zaw between the end of Afrāsyāb's usurpation and the advent of the founder of the Kayanid dynasty (on which, see *Mythe et épopée* II, p. 221).

19. P. 261.

20. Somewhat modified from Joseph Dunn, *The Ancient Irish Epic Tale Táin Bó Cualnge* (1914), pp. 2–3; cf. Windisch, p. 6.

21. A. and B. Rees, *Celtic Heritage*, pp. 130–31.

22. Windisch, p. 4.

23. Weisweiler, pp. 112–14, with discussion of the opinions on the meaning of Medb; see above, chap. 4, sec. 4.

24. Weisweiler, p. 113.

25. Ibid., p. 112.

26. Ibid., pp. 113–14. ó Máille, p. 144, interpreted one of the names for Connaught, *Cóiced (n-)Ólnecmacht*, as "The Province of the Drink of Powerlessness" (= intoxicating). But this explanation is contested: M. A. O'Brien, in *Ériu* 11(1932): 163–64, interprets *Cóiced ól nÉcmacht* as "the province beyond the impassable tract of land," Connaught being separated from Ulster by a nearly insuperable series of lakes and marshes, obstacles referred to in ancient literature.

27. ó Máille, p. 145.

28. See chap. 5, sec. 2, and chap. 2, sec. 1.

29. See chap. 2, sec. 1.

30. Ibid.

31. *Celtic Heritage*, p. 75, with references to Krappe and Coomaraswamy.

32. *Mythe et épopée* I, p. 122.

33. Paul-Émile Dumont, *L'Aśvamedha* (1927), pp. 152–54.

34. But Medb is not a courtesan; rather, she pays her partners. On this idle moral debate, see most recently the appropriate remarks of Françoise Le Roux, *Celticum* 15: 341–42.

35. See above, chap. 4, sec. 3.

36. This means of intoxicating is not foreign to Medb, of whom the *Dindṡenchas* in verse (ed. Edward Gwynn, IV [1913], p. 366) can say: "Such was the glory of Medb—and the excellence of her beauty—that two thirds of his valor he lost—every man who looked at her." F. Le Roux, *Celticum* 15: 343.

37. See chap. 5, sec. 3.

38. See chap. 4, sec. 1.

39. Most recently, see my *Archaic Roman Religion*, pp. 16–17, 582–85.

40. See *Mythe et épopée* II, part 1, developing a correspondence, concerning another aspect of the royal ideology, between India and two central parts of the Indo-European world, Scandinavia and Greece.

41. In Roman tradition, another quinquipartite "model" (in reality quadrupartite, with a subdivision) seems to have prevailed in an entirely different matter, where one would rather have expected a reference to the cardinal points. Varro, *De lingua latina* 5,33, says that the *augures publici* distinguished five types of terrains: *ager Romanus*, evidently at the center; *a. peregrinus*, certainly the nearest

to Rome (with its privileged variety *a. Gabinus*, which is indeed *peregrinus*, but has the *auspicia singularia*); *a. hosticus, a. incertus.*

42. See above, n. 2; O'Neill, p. 174 (transl. p. 175).

43. The Irish have proposed other etymologies.

44. The word is related to Indo-Iranian **yama* and to Old Scandinavian Ymir. The Vedic Yama and the Iranian Yima are also heroes in stories of incest with a sister (proposed by her and refused by him; or carried out; see the end of the Introduction, above). Lugaid had Cúchulainn for his master of arms, *Cóir Anman* §211 = *Irische Texte* III, 2 (1897), p. 374 (transl. p. 375). The taste for incest ran in the family, or at least in Clothra: she repeated the act with the son, Lugaid: *Eochadii f(eidhlech) filia Clothra mater Lugadii riab nderg, qui trium Finnorum filius; ipsa quoque mater Cremthanni, qui et eiusdem Lugadii filius,"* Standish O'Grady, *Silva Gadelica* II, p. 544 (= XXIII, IV, c).—Another etymology explains *emna* by the town *Emain* (Macha).

45. *Corob e Eochaid Feidleach rochuindid in itchi næmda cen mac indeog a athar for Erind e obrath, cor firad sin.*

46. In other arrangements of the material (in *Aided Medba*, for example, see below, sec. 4 and n. 54), this Conall Anglondach is not a son, but a brother of Eochaid Feidlech, the latter having no other sons than the Triplets.

47. Whitley Stokes, ed. and tr., "The Rennes Dindsenchas, 1st Supplement," *Revue Celtique* 16 (1895): 148–49 (149–50, transl.).

48. *Irische Texte* III, 2 (1897), §102, p. 330.

49. It is she, for example, who is asleep by the side of Conchobar in *Tochmarc Ferbe* (Windisch, ed. and tr., *Irische Texte*, III, 2 1897, pp. 472–73) when a very beautiful woman appears who announces the events of the *Táin Bó Cuailnge*.

50. See above, n. 2; O'Neill, pp. 174–76 (transl. pp. 175–77). For the concluding paragraph, the text reads:

> Is i cuis fa tuc rig Ereand na hingina sin do Concobar, air is le h-Eochaid Feidleach dothoit Fachna Fathach i cath Lithrechruaidi sa Corand, conad na eric tucad sin do, mailli re rigi n-Ulad do gabail do irreicin tar clandaib Rudraidi, conad he cet adbar comuachaid Thana Bo Cuailnge facbail Meadba ar Conchobar da a indeoin.

Cf. F. Le Roux, *Celticum* 15: 344.

51. As Mādhavī is handed over by her father to Gālava to avoid the dishonor of not giving the alms requested of him.

52. *Celticum* 15: 342–43, in her commentary on *Tochmarc Etaine* (see above, n. 46). According to this text, Eochaid has only three sons, the triplets, and three daughters, Eithne ("the Horrible"), Clothru, and Medb.

53. See above, chap. 4, end of sec. 2, and n. 26.

54. *Irische Texte* III, 2 (1897), §105, p. 332 (p. 333 transl.); the preceding paragraph explains the common name of the three brothers by *emain*, "twin"; see above, n. 44.

55. Livy, II, 32,7–12, and parallel texts.

56. *R̥V* 10,90,12.

57. P.-E. Dumont, *L'Aśvamedha* (1927), pp. 152–54, 271–72, 329–30; my *Archaic Roman Religion*, p. 225.

58. *The Pravargya, an Ancient Indian Iconic Ritual*, Deccan College, Poona, Building Centenary and Silver Jubilee Series, 58 (1968), pp. 11, 124–25.

59. This does not contradict what has been said above, sec. 3, on one particular point (the attenuation of the theme of "the Intoxicating" in Mādhavī).

60. Cf. what was said of the Ossetic heroine Satana in *Mythe et épopée* I, pp. 562–63.

Perspectives

1. See chap. 3, sec. 3, and chap. 3, sec. 5 (Yima); chap. 3, sec. 3 (Uparicara); and chap. 2, sec. 2 (Yayāti).

2. *Le type du premier homme* II, pp. 53–54.

3. Pp. 76–78, 99–101.

4. *The Destiny of the Warrior*, pp. 78–80, 103–4.

5. Most recently, see *Mythe et épopée* I, pp. 271–81; *The Destiny of the Warrior*, pp. 5–9; *Idées romaines* (1969), part 2, chap. 4.

6. For example, *Dionysius of Halicarnassus*, 2,56.

7. Livy, I, 31,8.

8. Ibid., I, 58–60.

9. For example, *ŚatapathaBrāhmaṇa* 5,1,5,1–6.

10. On the implications of this correspondence, see *Archaic Roman Religion*, pp. 16–17, 576–77, 582–83.

11. "Les cultes de la *regia*, les trois fonctions et la triade Juppiter Mars Quirinus," *Latomus* 13 (1954): pp. 129–39; *Archaic Roman Religion*, pp. 172–74). The *regia* has been excavated by Frank Brown: "The Regia," *Memoirs of the American Academy in Rome* 12 (1935): pp. 67–88, pl. iv–viii (cf. Giuseppe Lugli, *Roma antica, il centro monumentale* [1946], pp. 212–15: "Regia Pontificus"). More recent excavations have brought to light constructions of the seventh century (traces of a village) and of the sixth (traces of a small temple); the *regia* was constructed at the beginning of the fifth century; see Frank Brown, "New soundings in the Regia, the evidence from early Republic," *Les Origines de la république romaine, entretiens sur l'antiquité classique de la fondation Hardt* 13 (1967): pp. 47–64, and three plans. I owe a precise commentary on these plans to the kindness of Susan Dawney (of U.C.L.A.), who took part in the last excavations and who thinks that the fifth-century building reproduced an archaic plan (in the same manner that the wells, added later in the court, are archaic).

12. "Le *rex* et les *flamines maiores*," *Studies in the History of Religions: The Sacred Kingship*, (supplement to *Numen* IV), 8th International Congress of the History of Religions, Rome, April, 1955 (1959), pp. 407, 417; summarized in *Archaic Roman Religion*, pp. 583–85).

13. On Ops (duality of her festivals, epithet, connections with Quirinus, connections between the third and the first function), see the last essay of *Idées romaines*, pp. 289–303.

14. On Volcanus and the Volcanalia, see *Archaic Roman Religion*, pp. 320–21.

15. Tibullus, I,4,68; Ovid, *Tristes*, 2,24, etc.

16. *Volcanus (ignis): Aeneid*, V,662 (cf. 660) and IX,76; *deum genetrix Berecynthia, Mater, Cybele*, IX,92,94,108,117 and X,220; *aequoris deae, pelagi nymphae*; IX,102–3 and 220–21,231 *Cymodocea*, X,225; Aeneas, 219–61; on Aeneas as a prefiguration of Romulus, see *Mythe et épopée* I, pp. 337–422 ("Un dessein de Virgile").

17. "Ymlyc croth morwyn," in William John Gruffydd, *Math vab Mathonwy* (1928), p. 2. On the structure of the first part of this branch of the *Mabinogi* (the

children of Don), see *The Destiny of the Warrior*, pp. 144–45); on the structure of the second (the youthful exploits of Lleu), *Mythe et épopée* I, p. 189, n. 1.

18. *Snorra Edda Sturlusonar*, ed. Finnur Jónsson (1931), p. 39.

19. Ibid., p. 38.

20. Ibid., p. 67.

21. Ibid., p. 40.

22. In the episode of Balderus-Høtherus, III,ii,4 of Jørgen Olrik and Hans Ræder's edition (1931); on this episode, see my *From Myth to Fiction*, appendix 3.

23. *Snorra Edda Sturlusonar*, p. 38.

24. Cf. *Mythe et epopée* I, p. 234, n. 1.

25. It is indeed a question of the earth as the material of a kingdom (first function), and not of the earth as provider of nourishment (third function): see a similar situation, *Mythe et épopée* I, pp. 596–97. I do not see what elements of a Vegetationsgöttin would be contained in Gefjun's file (Jan de Vries, *Altgermanische Religionsgeschichte* II, pp. 329–31.

26. And even in the most euhemerized version (*Ynglingasaga*), when Óðinn emigrates from Denmark to Sweden, she remains in Zealand, marries Skjöldr, and thus finds herself at the origin of the Danish dynasty of the Skjöldungar.

INDEX